CHECK THE DECK

Integrated Composition Book for Young Students

by

LARRY LEWIN

edited by
Theresa Zigmond

The Stack the Deck Writing Program
Chicago, Illinois

Acknowledgments

"Ostrich in Love" from FABLES by Arnold Lobel. Copyright 1980 by Arnold Lobel. Reprinted by permission of Harper & Row, Publishers, Inc.

Excerpt from WILD AND WOOLY MAMMOTHS by Aliki (Thomas Y. Crowell) Copyright © 1977 by Aliki Brandenberg.

"From *Astronomy Encyclopedia*, published by Rand McNally, © Grisewood and Dempsey LTD. 1982. Reprinted by permission of Grisewood and Dempsey Ltd."

United Features Syndicate, Inc. for the March 1, 1988, Garfield Cartoon.

From *GOLDEN BOOK ENCYCLOPEDIA* ©Western Publishing Company, Inc. Used by permission.

THE FAR SIDE ©1985 Universal Press Syndicate.

Excerpt taken from *DINOSAUR STORY* by Joanna Cole. Copyright ©1974 by Joanna Cole. Reprinted by permission of William and Morrow & Company, Inc.

We would like to thank the following students from Eugene, Oregon, for allowing us to use samples of their writing in this text: Megan Force, Adriane Myers, Nathan McKay, Eric McGhee, Matthew Nelson, and Isaac Hernandez.

We would also like to thank the following teachers and administrators who inspired us with their ideas and offered practical suggestions for this revised edition: Elizabeth Moody, Joanne Paris, Sally Bickert, Mary Kalesse, Jane Johnson, and Sue Casey.

Special thanks to Theresa Zigmond for her helping in the design and layout and editing the revised edition, Nancy Happ for her valuable comments in with the original book, Jackie Nita for designing our new cover, and Penny Groves and Joe Koziarski for their illustrations.

ISBN 0-933282-29-X paperback
ISBN 0-933282-30-3 hard cover

This book is dedicated to my family:

Dad, Mom, Bob, and Linda

Table of Contents

Letter to Young Authors

Dear Student Author,

Welcome to **Check the Deck**.

I am very proud of this book because I wrote it for you. With twenty years of teaching students how to become better writers, I decided to write my ideas into this book. **Check the Deck** will help you to write better, and the ability to write well is one of the most important skills you can learn in school.

As a professional writer, I tried my best to make this book helpful and, at the same time, interesting. I want you to enjoy the activities so that writing becomes more fun for you.

Each chapter in this book will teach you a different way to write. You will learn how to write personal narratives, memos, reports, persuasive letters, and expository how-to-do papers. I wrote each chapter with lots of help for you -- I want you to be successful with many different types of writing.

There are many techniques in this book that will help you prepare to brainstorm, to write a rough draft, to re-write for improvements, and to share your writing with others. That is, I will teach you how to write like a pro!

Happy Writing!!

Best wishes,

Larry Lewin

Larry Lewin

Describing 1

Oral Language into Writing

COLORFUL WORDS

Welcome to **Check the Deck**. This book was written to help you become an **expert author**. Guess what? It's going to be very easy. You don't believe it? Just try doing these oral activities about words that add color to your ideas. Let's call these words **colorful words**. We use these words everyday to help describe or express ourselves.

Oral Activity 1: What kind. . .? Make up a word that tells what kind.

1. Dale ate a _____ peach.

    What kind of a peach? *fresh, mushy, sweet*.

2. Sheila likes _____ poodles.

3. I own two _____ snakes.

4. That _____ car is always parked there.

5. Those two circus clowns are very _____.

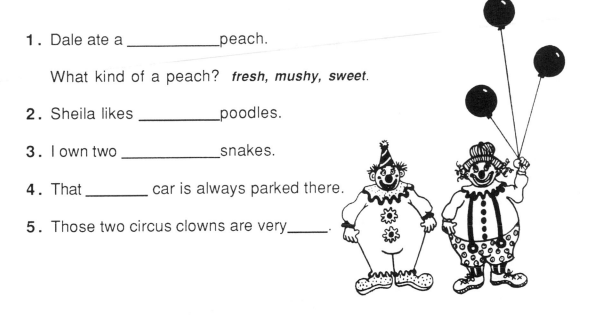

Oral Activity 2: Guess the Object--Raise your hand when you can guess the object your teacher describes. **Hint**: All the objects are found in this classroom. Listen carefully to the clues.

yellow, skinny, pointed, black tip, metal band--What is it?

1

COLORFUL WORDS

Words that describe people, animals, places, and things are **colorful words**, or adjectives.

Colorful words can show color. They also can describe shape and what kind. What is easier to see--a bear or a silly, dancing bear? How do the **bold words** make it easier to see the *thing* being described?

a **silly, dancing** bear
her **copper** snake
the **smiling** baby
a **crooked** fence

two **plump** rabbits
the **empty** plate
a **silver** spoon
lumpy potatoes

Oral Activity 3: Now you have some fun. **Expand** the following with **colorful words** in order to make them sound more exciting.

1. raccoon
2. swimming pool
3. prince
4. fire
5. computer

What colors?
What shape?
What kind?
What colors?
What kind?

Oral Activity 4: Pick the **best colorful words**. Tell why you like them best.

1. yellow, blond, lemony, golden, canary
2. bad, evil, nasty, naughty
3. slow, sluggish, pokey
4. dark, pitch-black, shadowy, gloomy
5. little, tiny, shrimpy, small, puny

Now add your own words to finish the list.

6. big, large, _____, _____, _____.
7. fast, speedy, _____, _____, _____.
8. stupid, silly _____, _____, _____.

Oral Activity 5: Use your imagination to select a **colorful word** that describes the person, animal, or thing in the sentences you hear your teacher read.

Example: Poor James has a _____ cold.

Taste, Feel, Sound, and Smell COLORFUL WORDS

Colorful words can also describe *taste*, *feel*, *sound*, and *smell*.
Here are some examples:

my **quiet** turtle
wet towel
shrill whistle
flowing river
sour cottage cheese
sticky candy bar
fresh baked bread

What other **colorful words** could you use to describe a
turtle, towel, whistle, river, cottage cheese, candy bar, and *bread?*

Oral Activity 6: In teams of four, **expand** each idea with at least
three **colorful words** that describe:

1. how a river **feels**
2. how a bakery **smells**
3. how a parakeet **sounds**
4. how an apple **tastes**
5. how hair **feels**

Use your dictionary or thesaurus if you need help.

Short Writing Assignment

Who Am I? Riddle

By using **colorful words**, you can play the *Who Am I?* riddle.
Describe yourself using **colorful words** so well that anyone
in your class can guess your name:

1. My hair color is _____.

2. My hair feels _____.

3. I would describe my size as _____.

4. My skin color is _____.

5. The color of my eyes is _____.

6. The color of my shirt or sweater is_____.

7. The jacket I usually wear looks _____.

8. The shoes I am wearing are _____.

9. Here's how I describe my backpack: _____.

10. My lunch box looks like _____.

A girl named Ingrid, who played this riddle game, wrote this
about herself.

> This is how I look. I am about as tall as Molly. Most of the
> time I wear brown shoes. I have brownish blonding hair.
> My hair is soft. My eyes are the color of grass and the sky
> mixed together. My skin is white. I wear different shirts
> most of the time.

The class guessed it was her. Now you try. Your teacher
might read your riddle to see if the class can **guess your name**.
She might even have you exchange riddles in small groups.

Practice 1: Finish these **combined** sentences by **expanding** with **colorful words**.

1. Her kangaroo is jumpy, brown, and _____.

2. Dickson loves rich, spicy, and _____food.

3. I hope to become a famous, popular, and _____actor.

4. You never wear clothes that are baggy, _____, and _____.

5. Giggly, _____, and _____ bears jump on my bed to wake me up.

Practice 2: **Combine** these short sentences by writing **colorful words** in a row. Be careful to copy the correct spelling.

1. My lobster is **green**. My lobster is **lovable**. My lobster is **strong**.

   My lobster is _____, _____, and _____.

2. Aunt Mimi's motorcycle was **shiny**. Aunt Mimi's motorcycle was **midnight blue**. Aunt Mimi's motorcycle was **powerful**.

   Aunt Mimi's motorcycle was _____, _____, and _____.

3. The island felt **hot**. The island felt **steamy**. The island felt **humid**.

4. Our neighbor Mr. Mertz looks **tall**. He looks **skinny**. He looks **young**.

5. When she was ignored by the other kids, Juanita felt **lonely**. Juanita felt **hurt**. Juanita felt **sad**.

An Easy Composing Rule

PUNCTUATING A SERIES

> **Punctuation Rule**: When you combine short, choppy sentences which repeat the same idea, you must put commas between the **colorful words**.

The kingdom seems rich. The kingdom seems busy.
The kingdom seems happy.

The kingdom seems _____, _____, and _____.

Example: The kingdom seems **rich, busy,** and **happy**.

Notice: If you have **three colorful words**, you need **two** commas.
The first comma goes **after** the first colorful word.
The last comma goes **before** the word *and*.

Practice 3: Tell where the **commas** belong in these **combined** sentences.

1. On our vacation we visited a tiny dusty and lonely town called Tingle.

2. A handsome strong and proud reindeer put on his antlers for show.

3. Dee Dee has bought her dad a purple silky long and expensive robe for his birthday.

Practice 4: Put in **commas** to separate **colorful words** in this short story.

Travels with Lindy

On her trip to Mexico, Lindy explored the Yucatan. This part of Mexico is dry and very warm. Her favorite places were the Mayan Indian ruins which are ancient sturdy and magnificent. For swimming and sunning, Lindy visited the beach. She was surprised to find the sand to be cool white and fine. Next time she plans to go to the markets to shop for hammocks baskets and shirts.

Writing with Style

SIMILES

Of course, you know that **colorful words** describe people, places, animals, and things.

Here is another way to describe someone or something.

- This works about as well **as** a three-wheeled skateboard.
- rare **as** a dinosaur
- This soup is hot **as** lava.
- nervous **as** a crocodile at the dentist
- fragile **like** a piece of chalk
- blue **as** the ocean
- hot **as** the sun in a microwave oven
- These crackers taste **like** sawdust.
- lonesome **as** a puppy in a cage

These are called **similes**. They always use *like* or *as* when they compare two things.

Here are some often-used similes. Match them.

1. happy *as* a	**a.** bear
2. hungry *as* a	**b.** hawk
3. quick *like* a	**c.** glass
4. white *as*	**d.** lark
5. watched *like* a	**e.** new snow
6. smooth *as*	**f.** fox

Practice 5: You can invent better **similes** than these. Let your imagination be as *free as a shooting star.*

1. After the dentist told me that I had no cavities, I was as happy
   as _____.

2. Space traveler Captain Rhonda Rocket was hungry
   as _____.

3. We better watch the baby closely. She's quick
   like _____.

4. Adam stared in shock as the oven floated out the door. His face
   turned white *as* _____.

5. The new puppy will chew the furniture, so we watch her
   like _____.

6. At night the frog pond is as smooth
   as _____.

Practice 6: Imagine and describe how you would feel if you were:

1. *like* a cat in a fish store
2. *like* Santa Claus on the day
   after Christmas
3. *like* a hippo under the bed
4. *like* a cowgirl without a horse
5. *like* a banana at a gorilla's picnic

A **SIMILE** sounds even better when one jumps out at you from a story. Then it is as surprising *as finding a diamond in a Corn Flakes box.* Read this short story about Felice, the Speedster. See if you find a **sneaky simile**.

Felice, the Speedster

Baby-sitting is the only job my twelve-year-old brother Harry can get. He can't stand waking up early, so a paper route is out of the question. He baby-sits for a little adorable and active kid named Felice.

Sometimes I go over to Felice's house with Harry to help out. The last time we were baby-sitting Felice, she was very active. I mean, this baby can crawl around forever. Harry warned me that we better watch her closely. He said she was as quick as a cat heading for an open tuna fish can.

Two micro-seconds later she crawled so fast right out the door that Harry and I both had to chase after her. Pulling her back to the couch, Harry suddenly decided getting up early for a paper route wouldn't be so bad.

Practice 7: Short Writing Assignment: Choose your favorite **simile** from **Practice 6** or write one of your own. Make up a short story using it. You can invent make-believe characters or use real ones. Then draw a picture of your simile. Read your story to a partner.

Major Writing Assignment

DESCRIPTIVE WRITING--NEIGHBORHOOD VACATION

STAGE ONE: PREWRITING

Student Learning Objectives

In this paper, you will:

1. describe a neighborhood place using **colorful words**.

2. describe something using a **simile**.

3. use commas with **colorful words** in a series.

Helpful Drills

Colorful words have opposites, which are called antonyms. In order to write about a place you've been to, it will be helpful to use the opposites of some **colorful words**.
Here is some practice:

square------------------------round

sour---------------------------sweet

sharp--------------------------dull

wet----------------------------dry

mean--------------------------kind

Practice 8: Write an interesting opposite for these **colorful words**.

1. scream
2. lovely
3. smooth
4. friendly
5. bored

6. charming
7. sharp
8. alert
9. powerful
10. big

14

Practice 9: Change the **colorful words** into opposites to make them unappealing-- yukky.

> **Example**: For lunch everyone feasted on **fresh** fruit.
>
> For lunch everyone feasted on **smelly, rotten** fruit.

1. The **sandy** beach stretched for miles.
2. I found the inhabitants of Borky Island to be **kind-hearted**.
3. In Mushton **beautiful** flowers grow all year.
4. A favorite pastime in Peabody Point is **planting** flowers.
5. Mostly they live in **sturdy** houses.

Practice 10: Now write three sentences of your own about an everyday place you have visited. Each sentence must have **colorful words**. Then trade papers with a partner and change the **colorful words** into their antonyms (opposites).

Congratulations! You have finished the helpful drills. Now you are ready for the first major writing assignment of *Check the Deck*.

Writing Prompt

Have you ever seen a travel brochure? They are fancy printed booklets used to advertise a nice place to visit. To catch your attention and urge you to come visit, the travel brochure uses **colorful words** to describe the place or location.

Your first major writing assignment is to write a travel brochure advertising a place near where you live. Instead of describing a fancy place like Disneyland or The White House, you will write a travel brochure for a common place in your neighborhood, like the corner store, a park, or even your own house.

It is your *purpose* as the writer to describe your neighborhood place using **colorful words** to make it seem so fancy, fabulous, and fascinating that someone taking a vacation would actually choose to come visit.

Think Sheet

A **think sheet** is a useful tool to help you gather your thoughts. It helps you brainstorm and keep on track.

On the next page, use the **think sheet** to help you *focus* and concentrate on your content and *organize* your travel brochure.

Think Sheet--Neighborhood Vacation Brochure

1. What is the name of the neighborhood place you will describe? (Make it sound very fancy and important!)

   _____

2. Where is it located? Give clear directions to get there.

   _____

3. Write three **colorful words** in a row that describe this place.

   _____

4. Who are some fabulously interesting people to meet there?

   _____

5. What terrific activities can visitors do there?

   _____

   _____

6. Who should the visitor bring along on this trip?

   _____

7. Write a **simile** describing the people, their homes, the weather, or the great activities.

   _____

STAGE TWO: WRITING THE FIRST DRAFT

You are ready to begin writing your travel brochure about the fabulous *Neighborhood Vacation*. Use the ideas from your **think sheet** to get you started. As you write, you can change your ideas from the **think sheet** if you get a better or new idea. Write your story as quickly as you can without worrying about getting it perfect. Just write. This is called a **first draft**, a **rough draft**, or a **sloppy copy**.

When you write a **sloppy copy**, it is not perfect.

- Guess how to spell hard words. Circle them to check later. Then go on. *Guess and Go spelling*.

- Write quickly. Handwriting doesn't have to be your neatest now.

- Not all parts must be perfect. You can work on the sloppy copy later.

To make your story easier to work on later:

- Write in pencil.

- Skip every other line.

- When you finish, go back and number each sentence.

STAGE THREE: REWRITING

Sometimes your first draft is pretty good, so you will continue working on it. Making changes for improvement is called **rewriting**. All authors must rewrite to improve their work. They can fix up weak parts, misspelling, sloppiness, or other problems. They work alone or get help from others.

Rewriting Alone

Here is a good way to fix up your brochure story **by yourself**.

After you have finished the **sloppy copy**, read it to yourself aloud to look and listen for parts you want to change. Maybe you forgot to name a character. Perhaps you missed putting in commas between a series of **colorful words**. Maybe you want to put in an antonym where it fits. Maybe you can rearrange some parts, so your brochure sounds better. Maybe you can **combine** short, choppy sentences.

You can write the changes on your paper. After all, it is a **sloppy copy**. This is called *messifying* your brochure. Use this checklist to guide you.

Name_____

Travel Brochure Checklist

1. What is the name of my neighborhood place? _____

   _____

2. Where is it located? _____

   _____

3. What are at least **3 colorful words** in a row that I used to describe this place? _____

   _____

4. What are the names of any interesting people who live or work there? _____

   _____

5. What are the thrilling activities to do there? _____

   _____

6. Whom do I recommend a visitor bring along? _____

   _____

7. Here is my great **simile**: _____

   _____

   _____

Rewriting with Help

Here is a plan to discover ways to improve your neighborhood travel description with help.

First, you can read your brochure to your teacher who wants to hear it. You two can talk it over to see if you can make your brochure more interesting. Your teacher becomes your **editor**.

You can also share your brochure with a friend and see what he thinks of your story. From your description, does your reader think people would like to visit your neighborhood? Why or why not? You might need to **expand** with more details.

Then you make any changes you think will make your story *better*. Use the same guide questions from the checklist.

STAGE FOUR: PUBLISHING

Share your neighborhood travel adventure with others.
Design a travel brochure advertising all the great reasons
to visit your special place.

First, triple-fold the paper into a brochure. Next, carefully
copy your improved draft into the columns. Finally, be sure to
add some colorful illustrations showing what the place looks like.

Quick Review

Remember that good writers **combine** short, choppy sentences
into longer ones. **Combining** is your first **writer's vocabulary word**.
This skill will help you to rewrite your sentences as you begin to
revise.

Also, remember to expand with **colorful words** to make your
ideas easier for your reader to see.

Stay Tuned

In **Chapter 2** you will learn how to solve a problem for Super
Turkey. Who??

Imaginative Problem Solving 2

Oral Language into Writing

FLEXIBLE WORDS

Chi Chi is a very talented anteater who wants to try to do everything. She thinks she is a person. Tell what Chi Chi does:

Chi Chi **pets** worms.

She didn't do a very good job, though. She squished them. She felt badly, so now:

Chi Chi **worms** pets. (Tell what she does now.)

How did the sentences change?

Chi Chi pets worms.
Chi Chi worms pets.

Pets can mean both   **1)** animals kept by people and
2) to gently stroke

Worms can mean both   **1)** small, legless, wiggly animal and
2) to remove worms from animal's stomach

NOUNS AND VERBS

Some words in English can be both **nouns** and **verbs**.
A noun is any person, place, or thing.

> **Nouns** are *things*, such as houses, trails, and tests.
> **Nouns** are *people*, such as babies, friends, and guards.
> **Nouns** are *animals*, such as bats, flies, worms, and pets.
> **Nouns** are *places*, such as schools, farms, and stores.

Verbs are *action words*,
such as **stains** her shirt,
or **flies** a plane,
or **bats** a ball,
or **worms** a puppy.

Oral Activity 1: Tell whether the **bold-faced** words are nouns
or verbs.

1. a. The **bats** lay beside home plate. What are bats?
   b. Mr. Clone **bats** a home run. What does Mr. Clone
      do when he bats the ball?

2. a. She put her **hands** inside her pockets. What are hands?
   b. Lisa, please **hand** me the screwdriver. What does Lisa do
      when she hands a screwdriver to her mom?

24

FLIP-FLOPPING WORDS

When you **flip-flop** one of these words, the meaning of the sentence changes.

> **1.** Chi Chi *cooks* **squashes**.

> **2.** Chi Chi *squashes* **cooks**.

Tell what the difference is between sentences 1 and 2.

Oral Activity 2: For each numbered pair of sentences, first tell what Chi Chi is doing. Then switch the words to fill in the blank, and explain what she does next.

1. Chi Chi bats flies.
   Chi Chi flies _____.
   _____

2. Chi Chi paints ships.
   Chi Chi ships_____.
   _____

3. Chi Chi rocks babies.
   Chi Chi babies_____.
   _____

4. Chi Chi treats burns.
   Chi Chi burns_____.
   _____

Simple Sentence Combining

COMBINING WITH GLUE WORDS

You learned in **Chapter 1** how to join three or four short, choppy sentences into one longer, more interesting sentence by using **colorful words** in a series. Remember?

The recycled bottles are **green**, **brown**, and **clear**.

In your **writer's vocabulary**, this is called **combining** sentences. Writers use words such as **before**, **after**, **when**, and **because** to glue ideas together. They are called **glue words**.

Chi Chi treats burns. Chi Chi burns treats.
After Chi Chi treats burns, she burns treats.

Chi Chi takes a nap. Chi Chi plays cards.
Before Chi Chi takes a nap, she plays cards.

Chi Chi marks spots. Chi Chi finds the trail.
Because Chi Chi marks spots, she finds the trail.

Practice 1: Combine these short sentences using **before**, **after**, **when**, or **because**.

1. Chi Chi made a mistake. Chi Chi got fired.
   After Chi Chi made a mistake, she _____ _____.

2. Chi Chi paints ships. Chi Chi bats flies.
   Before Chi Chi _____ _____, she _____ _____.

3. Chi Chi eats chips. Chi Chi gets hiccups.

When_____ _____, she _____ _____.

4. Chi Chi loses needles. Chi Chi wears boots.

_____

5. Chi Chi brushes her teeth. Chi Chi drinks ant juice.

_____

Here is another example:

> Soapsie earns money. Soapsie buys a pair of inline skates.
> **After** Soapsie earns money, she buys a pair of inline skates.

If the same person (or animal or thing) is doing two actions, you can **combine** the two short sentences.

> **My dad** cooks a Chinese dinner. **My dad** washes the dishes.

- begin with a **glue word**
- use *he, she, they, we,* or *it* to replace the name
- remove the ending period and next capital letter

> **After** my dad cooks a Chinese dinner, ___he___ washes the dishes.

27

Practice 2: Combine these sentences using **after**, **before**, **when**, or **because**. Use either *she*, *he*, *it*, or *they*.

1. Tobie swallowed a marble. Tobie put a marble in his mouth.

2. Three kitties lie in the sun. The kitties are lazy.

3. The vacuum cleaner was making a grinding noise. The vacuum cleaner broke.

4. Deven read *Charlotte's Web*. Deven made a book poster.

Short Writing Assignment

Pick your favorite pair of Chi Chi's jobs from **Oral Activity 2**. Write a short story about her. Your story should *focus* on:

- describing her first job
- explaining the problem she had with it
- describing how she got her second job
- explaining if she does it well or not

Be sure to use your first **writer's vocabulary** word and **combine** some sentences using:

- three **colorful words** in a series
- a **glue word** joining two short sentences

This is a **sloppy copy**, so you can:

- write in pencil.
- skip lines.
- use *Guess and Go spelling*. Circle words you question.
- do not worry about neatness--must be readable.

Here is a sample story about two of Chi Chi's jobs from **page 26**:
Chi Chi treats burns. Chi Chi burns treats.

Treat or Trick

Chi Chi was a very unhappy, little anteater. Actually, she was depressed. Every Halloween children would dress up in their costumes for trick or treating. And every year people would mistake her for a kid dressed in an anteater costume. They would say, "Look at this silly kid dressed like an anteater!" So Chi Chi took a job **burning the treats** to put an end to it.

Of course, all the children were sad, unhappy, and disappointed. They told Chi Chi not to ruin Halloween. After they promised not to laugh at her anymore, she agreed. She found a better job at the hospital **treating burns**. She enjoyed this work so much that she applied to medical school to become a doctor.

Which sentence begins with a **glue word**?
Which sentence contains three **colorful words** in a row?

An Easy Composing Rule

PUNCTUATING GLUE WORDS

You learned in **Chapter 1** that when you join sentences with **colorful words**, you must add **commas**. Remember? How many commas do you add with three **colorful words**? How many for four **colorful words**? Eight?

Now you've learned how to join sentences which begin with **glue words**. You must use **one comma**. It is placed where the short, choppy sentences are joined:

Example: Since Chi Chi farms soil, she sprouts beans.
   Glue word 1st sentence **Comma** 2nd sentence.

_____ _____, _____.

Practice 3: Tell where the **comma** belongs in these **combined** sentences.

   1. Before I will loan you my cobra you must learn its diet.

   2. Because Ms. Willow brought a car we get a ride home.

   3. After the rain stops falling the birds will return.

   4. Since smoking is bad for his health my brother quit.

Practice 4: Read your Chi Chi story again. Find the sentence that uses a **glue word**. Put in a **comma** where it belongs.

Writing with Style

USING PERSONIFICATION IN STORIES

Chi Chi is a clever anteater. Anteaters can do many things, but the jobs we invented for Chi Chi are make-believe. She couldn't really **worm pets**, **treat a burn**, or **rock babies**. Only people can do these things. When we make believe that an animal or an object can behave like a person, it is called **personification**.

Birds of prey know they're cool.

1. What animals are acting like a person?
2. What are the animals doing?
3. Could an animal really do that?

31

Practice 5: Read this fable by Arnold Lobel to find **personification** of an ostrich. For every day of the week, find what the ostrich did like a human.

THE OSTRICH IN LOVE

On Sunday the Ostrich saw a young lady walking in the park. He fell in love with her at once. He followed behind her at a distance, putting his feet in the very places where she had stepped.

On Monday the Ostrich gathered violets as a gift to his beloved. He was too shy to give them to her. He left them at her door and ran away, but there was a great joy in his heart.

On Tuesday the Ostrich composed a song for his beloved. He sang it over and over. He thought it was the most beautiful music he had ever heard.

On Wednesday the Ostrich watched his beloved dining in a restaurant. He forgot to order supper for himself. He was too happy to be hungry.

On Thursday the Ostrich wrote a poem to his beloved. It was the first poem he had every written, but he did not have the courage to read it to her.

On Friday the Ostrich bought a new suit of clothes. He fluffed his feathers, feeling fine and handsome. He hoped that his beloved might notice.

On Saturday the Ostrich dreamed that he was waltzing with his beloved in a great ballroom. He held her tightly as they whirled around and around to the music. He awoke feeling wonderfully alive.

On Sunday the Ostrich returned to the park. When he saw the young lady walking there, his heart fluttered wildly, but he said to himself. "Alas, it seems that I am much too shy for love. Perhaps another time will come. Yet, surely, this has been a week well spent."

Love can be its own reward.

Practice 6: Explain the **personification** in these sentences. What is the animal doing *like a person*?

1. Siggie Salmon swam to the video store to rent *Free Willy*.
   Could a salmon *swim*?
   Could a salmon *enter a video store*?
   Could a salmon *rent a videotape*?
2. I get so angry when I catch my cat in my bedroom using my headphones to listen to my tapes.

33

3. Mr. Dibbs, a peaceful crocodile, went to the dentist because he had a toothache.

4. Sal's lobster got a job working as an electrician snipping wires.

5. Garfield tricked Jon by locking him out of the house.

6. Before Goldilocks arrived, the three bears made porridge.

7. Yogi Bear and BooBoo hopped into the park ranger's truck and took off.

8. Turning to Bullwinkle Moose, Rocky the Flying Squirrel said, "Well, you did it again."

Personification is an animal behaving like a human. The animal can be:

- talking
- dressing in clothes
- thinking
- shopping

Practice 7: Which sentences have **personification** and which do not?

1. My parakeet won't get off the phone.

2. The horse in the pasture watches a car drive by.

3. A bald eagle bought a golf cap to keep its head from sun burning.

4. Baby alligators at the zoo took a little swim.

5. The caterpillar bought a new sweater with extra sleeves.

34

Practice 8: Your turn. Make these animals act like people. Pick three. Write a sentence with **personification** in it.

1. baby mice
2. lonely dinosaur
3. three chickens in a boat

4. a spider and a fly
5. your dog (or cat)
6. giant panda named Vinnie

Practice 9: Short Writing Assignment: Choose your favorite **personification** from **Practice 8**. Write a short story using it. You can make up names for the animals and have them talk. Read your story to a partner.

Major Writing Assignment

IMAGINATIVE WRITING--SOLVING A PROBLEM

STAGE ONE: PREWRITING

Student Learning Objectives

You will write a story about Super Turkey. Your story will:

1. make the animal **solve a problem**.

2. have a **beginning**, a **middle**, and an **ending**.

3. combine sentences using **glue** and **colorful words**.

4. use **personification**.

Writing Prompt

In many comics, cartoons, and even books, animals are made-up to be **Super Heroes**. Animals like Mighty Mouse, Wonder Dog, Karate Kat, Rocky the Flying Squirrel, and Ninja Turtles do amazing acts. In your next story you will use your imagination and write about Super Turkey who has super powers. The situation should be dangerous. Super Turkey comes to the rescue to solve the problem. Your story should have a beginning, a middle, and an ending.

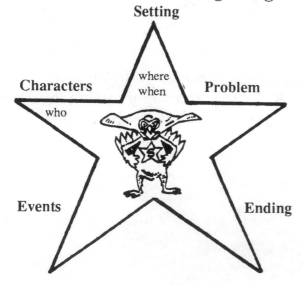

A newspaper reported that a super creature, Super Turkey, has been flying around the world helping people and animals in trouble. It has been spotted as far away as China. It is always wearing a yellow cape and goggles.

36

Think Sheet--Super Turkey's Problem

1. Why is Super Turkey needed? (What dangerous problem or mystery?)

   _____

   _____

   _____

   _____

2. Where does the story take place? _____

   _____

3. What does it look like? (Use **colorful words**.)

   _____

   _____

4. Who are the other characters in the story?

   _____

   _____

5. How do the other characters feel about Super Turkey?

   _____

   _____

6. How does Super Turkey solve the problem or mystery?

   _____

   _____

STAGE TWO: WRITING THE FIRST DRAFT

Follow your **think sheet** to write a **first draft--sloppy copy--** of your Super Turkey problem-solving story. Use your *story star* to plunge into the action or to set the scene. Tell your reader what is happening right away.

- Write in pencil.

- Number each sentence.

- Skip every other line.

- *Guess and Go* for hard spelling.

- Handwriting just neat enough to read.

- Not every part of the story must be perfect.

STAGE THREE: REWRITING

When a **rough draft** is pretty good, it should be worked on more to make it really great. One way to improve a **rough draft** is to read it aloud to yourself like you did with the **Neighborhood Vacation** story in **Chapter 1**.

- Read slowly hearing every word.

- Mark any mistakes you find.

- Add anything you need.

- Cross out anything you don't like.

Reading to Someone Else

Another way to fix up a **rough draft** is to read it to someone else. In **Chapter 1** your teacher listened to your story. This time you will have your partner listen to you.

- Read your story aloud to your partner.

- Ask your partner to answer the questions from the checklist.

- Then you listen to your partner's story.

- You answer the questions that follow.

- Trade stories to check the answers from the checklist. Discuss your answers with your partner.

Proofreading Practice: Class Activity

Before you work with a partner, let's practice proofreading. Read this news story with your class. Then answer the six checklist questions on page **41**.

Pinkietown, New Mexico, was invaded by a no-good band of rattlesnakes. Lean, mean, and bored, these snakes loved trouble. They slithered over to the shopping mall and blocked the entrance by shaking their rattles at anyone who tried to enter. Business stopped. People were afraid.

Luckily for the town, a mild-mannered turkey arrived to compete in the Power Ping Pong Contest. She waddled over to the mall to purchase a new, personalized, power ping pong paddle. Before she reached the entrance, she sensed trouble.

Hiding behind an RV in the parking lot, the turkey quickly changed into an orange cape and pink goggles. She approached the rattlesnakes. They were not impressed by a turkey in an orange cape and pink goggles. One of them (known as Skinny) asked, "Don't you know Halloween is over? Your costume looks like a rotten orange in a pink garbage can."

She replied, "Don't you know Super Turkey cares not that Halloween is over? Your rattles look like smoke from a fire."

Skinny checked his rattles. They were smoking. But when he tried to rattle them, they went "gobble, gobble" instead. Within ten seconds the band of snakes slid away from the entrance and quickly left town.

The next day Super Turkey won the contest and qualified for the national tournament in Table Tennis, Tennessee.

Super Turkey Checklist

1. What is the animal Super Hero's name?_____

_____

2. What does it look like?_____

_____

_____

3. Write the three **colorful words** you found in a series:

_____   _____

_____

4. Write the sentence which begins with a **glue word** in it. Underline the **glue word**.

_____

_____

5. List three human actions (**personification**):

_____

_____

_____

6. What problem is solved at the end?_____

_____

_____

STAGE FOUR: PUBLISHING

You have worked hard on this story. It should be shared with children who would love to hear it. Why not copy your story with any changes onto a fresh piece of paper? How about drawing a picture of this Super Hero? Then you can share it with other students.

Skills Summary

Here are some ways to use your **writer's vocabulary skills** when you revise a composition:

1. If too many of your sentences are short and choppy, **combine** some of them.

2. If too many of your sentences begin with the same words, **combine** them by using a glue word.

3. If your audience wants more information as they read your story, **expand** with more support.

Stay Tuned

In **Chapter 3** you will become a detective. Find out why.

Reporting

Oral Language into Writing

CREATING NEW NAMES

Do you think that your grandparents ever talked about **skateboards** when they were young? Why not? What about **tacos**? Yes or no? Did cave men and women mention the word **telephone**? Of course they didn't. They had no need for it.

Words come from a need--a need to name a *thing* being used. We now have plastic equipment with wires that let us talk to someone far away. They are named **telephones**. Those low boards with rollerskate wheels that kids ride are named **skateboards**. Nowadays many people enjoy **tacos**. New words can come from science (television), borrowed from another language (taco), or invented to match the new thing (skate + board).

Oral Activity 1: Here are some newly invented words for products available in the past. Can you tell what these things are and how they work?

1. inline skates
2. compact disc (CD)
3. cellular phone
4. modem
5. fax machine

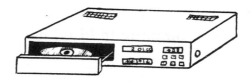

Can you think of other new names?

Oral Activity 2: Make up a name for these new inventions that haven't been invented yet.

1. skateboard with a sail

2. hairstyle that is shaped like animals

3. book with recorded characters' voices from a mini-speaker

4. pencil that copies handwriting into printed type

5. lunch box that cooks food inside of it

Short Writing Assignment

Pick your favorite new word from **Oral Activity 1, 2,** or one of your own words and write a paragraph about it. Your *purpose* is to convince a company to build it:

- explain what the new thing is

- describe what it looks like

- tell when or how it's used

Simple Sentence Combining

COMBINING WITH COMPOUND SUBJECTS

The light bulb is an invention that makes life easier.
The washing machine is an invention that makes life easier.

Many inventions have made life easier. Why not **combine** the two sentences to make them into one?

The light bulb and washing machine are inventions that make life easier.

Combining saves us from writing the words *invention that make life easier* twice. We **subtracted** those five words. Of course, *is* must be changed to *are* for agreement. **Subtracting** is another **writer's vocabulary** word.

The two inventions are called **subjects** of the sentence. Subjects tell the **doer** of the sentence. Two subjects are called compound subjects. (two DOERS)

Doer   Doer   Does

<u>Mickey</u> and <u>Minnie</u> <u>are moving</u> to Arizona without Pluto.

Practice 1: Name the two **DOERS** (subjects) in these sentences.

1. Skateboards and bicycles move people down the streets.
2. Pluto and Jupiter revolve around the sun in our solar system.
3. Silvio makes new friends in the neighborhood. [**tricky**]
4. Mzxcf and Jjobu will fly to Earth next week.
5. Radios and televisions bring us the news.

Practice 2: Your turn. **Combine** these sentences into longer ones using **compound subjects**. You may have to change a word to match two things after you **subtract** some words. For example:

> Deb wants to learn Spanish. + Troy wants to learn Spanish.
> **Deb** and **Troy** want to learn Spanish.

1. Howie will paint the garage.
   I will paint the garage.

2. Apples have vitamin C in them.
   Oranges have vitamin C in them.

3. Dad shampooed the family room rug.
   Uncle Ziggy shampooed the family room rug.

4. Mom loves to bake sugar cookies.
   Maria loves to bake sugar cookies.

5. Elmore races his new remote control car. Zelda races her new remote control car.

6. Sunlight is important to plant growth.
   Food is important to plant growth.

7. Count, our dog, chewed the steak bone. Felix, the cat, chewed the steak bone.

Practice 3: Make up sentences for these compound subjects.

1. Buff and Biff (two buffaloes in a grocery store)

2. a matador and a bull (the bull has the cape)

3. shoes and socks (under a bed)

An Easy Composing Rule

CORRECTING FRAGMENTS

Do you remember what a **compound subject** is? What do you think a simple subject is? Which sentence has a compound subject? A simple subject?

> Veggies and rice are a good dinner at my house.
> Veggies are a good dinner at my house.

A compound subject has **two** or **more** subjects:

> **Tammi** and **JoJo** never talk to each other.

A simple subject has just **one** subject:

> **Tammi** never talks anymore.

What if you read a sentence with no subject?

> Are a good dinner at my house.
> Was walking a giant fish downtown.
> Sat under a tree on Thursday.
> Asked me for 15 cents.

They make no sense, do they? A *sentence* with no subject is no sentence at all. It's a lowly **fragment**.

Practice 4: Tell which of the following are sentences (**S**) and which are fragments (**F**).

1. Sally ate all the corn chips as usual.
2. Forgot to enter the lottery.
3. Swallows marshmallows beside the campfire.
4. Bats and balls were left on the playground.
5. Were invented in the last century.

Practice 5: Fix these **fragments** by making up a simple and a compound subject for them. **Expand**.

1. Drops crumbs to the birds in the park.
   a. _____ drops crumbs to the birds in the park.
   b. _____ and _____ drop crumbs to the birds in the park.

2. Was screaming and jumping on the bed!
   a. _____.
   b. _____ and _____.

3. Sits on the couch with Mick.
   a. _____.
   b. _____.

Special Fragment Tip: On a 3 x 5 or 4 x 6 index card, write the words:

I Believe That

Every time you want to see if a group of words is a fragment, pull out your card. Read the words *I Believe That* in front of the words you are checking. If the idea makes sense, it is a **sentence**. If the words sound confusing, it is probably a **fragment**.

Example: *Are baking chocolate chip cookies.*
           I Believe That *are baking chocolate chip cookies.*

Sounds confusing, right? This is a **fragment**. Try this one:

Example: *The Munsters are baking chocolate chip cookies.*
           I Believe That *the Munsters are baking chocolate chip cookies.*

Sounds okay, right? This group of words is a **sentence**.

Writing with Style

VOICE IN WRITING

Can you recognize your teacher's voice? How about your favorite cartoon character's voice on television? If the president called you on the phone, would you know his voice? Even if you couldn't see these people, you probably would know who was talking.

Voice in writing is the same. You can hear the author talking to you when you read the words.

Practice 6: Listen to your teacher read you three stories. What kind of voices do you hear?

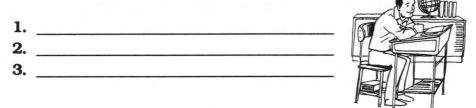

1. _____
2. _____
3. _____

Good writing lets the reader **hear the writer's voice**. Even though the writer is far away, the reader can hear the writer's words come off the printed page.

Practice 7: Remember the **Super Turkey** story? Here it is written in a newspaper **reporter's voice**. Read it with your class.

Super Turkey To The Rescue

(Pinkietown, New Mexico)**1.** After months of terror, the residents of this city were rescued today from a band of no-good rattlesnakes known as *The Slime*. **2.** Slithering into town last June, these repulsive reptiles had taken over the shopping mall by blocking the entrances and shaking their rattles at any humans who tried approaching.

3. Then yesterday, a mild-mannered turkey, who claimed only to have been shopping for a new ping pong paddle, arrived at the mall.
4. Quickly sizing up the dangerous situation, she quickly transformed into Super Turkey by hiding behind a huge RV in the parking lot and changing into a flashing orange cape and matching pink goggles.

5. Shoppers later reported Super Turkey confronted the rattlers blocking the front door.
6. They were not impressed by a turkey in an orange cape and pink goggles.

7. One rattlesnake, later identified as Skinny, was quoted as saying, "Hey, Turkey, don't you realize Halloween is over?
8. Your costume looks like an orange rotting in a pink garbage can."

9. Witnesses report that Super Turkey narrowed her eyes and focused on the snake's rattles for several seconds before smoke billowed. **10.** The angry rattler shook its rattles as a danger warning, but the crowd burst into laughter when they went "gobble, gobble" instead.

11. Within ten seconds the fearsome snake band had disappeared out of the city.

12. Super Turkey was surrounded for interviews, but she stated that it was time to change into her jogging suit and enter the ping pong tournament in Table Tennis, Tennessee.

On your own paper, write down some words that sound like a newspaper reporter.

1.   **4.**

2.   **5.**

3.

Now go back to **Chapter 2 (pages 39-40)** and read the original version. How does it sound different?

Here is the **Super Turkey** story again, but this time it is told by a police detective investigating it. Hear the **detective's voice**?

Police Report

I received a call at 5:19 P.M. to proceed to the Shopping Mall to investigate a complaint. Witnesses near the front entrance testified that a band of rattlesnakes (known to residents as *The Slime*) had blocked the entrance at approximately 4:30 - 5:00 P.M. The snakes were described as making menacing noises, shaking their rattles, and generally bothering shoppers.

There was no sign of the alleged band of snakes. However, I did discover a burned mark on the pavement and some ashes that I have sent to the lab for identification.

Witnesses stated that the snake band was driven off by a turkey identified as Super Turkey. Its description was given as:

      2 - 3 years old

      typical feathers and coloring

      unusual dress: orange cape and pink goggles

      barefoot

According to the witnesses at the scene, this Super Turkey ignited the rattles of one of the band members. Witnesses were unable to describe how.

52

Practice 8: On your own paper, write down the words from the **Police Report** that sound like a detective is talking.

1.
2.
3.
4.
5.

Voice is easy to put into your writing. Decide who you want to sound like, and then choose words that match.

my dada = little kid   my dad = other child
my daddy = child   my father = older still

Practice 9: Who would sound like this?

1. Dada!
2. Hi, Daddy!
3. Hey, Dad!
4. Hello, Father!
5. What's happening, Pop!
6. That mine.
7. That's mine.
8. The witness stated that it belonged to her.
9. That is my possession.
10. If you can't share it, I'll put it away, so neither of you can play with it.

Major Writing Assignment

PREDICTING AN OUTCOME
Solving a Mystery in a Detective Report

STEP ONE: PREWRITING

Student Learning Objectives

In this paper you will:

1. write a **detective report** with supporting evidence.

2. use a detective's **voice**.

3. combine sentences using **compound subjects**.

4. avoid **fragments**.

Writing Prompt

You are a detective hired to solve a puzzling case. A sixteen-year-old girl named Julia X. has been charged with stealing merchandise from Tubie's Sporting Goods Store. She says she is innocent and has hired you to find the true thief.

Read the mystery which follows. Watch carefully for hints that will help you solve the mystery. Did Julia do it, or was it someone else? Then you will write a detective report. Your report should explain who the real thief is and which clues you discovered to help you solve the mystery.

Julia X. works for Tubie's Sporting Goods Store as a salesperson. She was thrilled to get the job because she needed money. Julia loves sports, especially basketball.

Her next-door neighbor, Sam Slade, who is a senior at the high school and on the boy's basketball team, wanted to know if basketballs were on sale at Tubie's. He and Julia had been friends since grade school. They played basketball together for years on his driveway basketball court. Julia told him she didn't know of any sale coming up. She thought how nice it would be to get a new basketball for Sam since she had used his old one, too. She also knew his birthday was in three weeks.

Julia loved working at Tubie's. Everyday after school from 3:00 to 6:00 P.M. and most Saturdays she waited on customers to sell them jogging shoes, golf clubs, swimming suits, baseball bats, and many other sporting goods.

She was a good worker and very careful. The boy who had the job before her was fired because he carelessly lost the key to the back door several months ago.

When Julia arrived at Tubie's last Tuesday, she was surprised that the back door was unlocked. Mr. Tubie would be upset by this, but Julia figured that maybe he himself had forgotten to lock it. Mr. Tubie was often forgetful.

Last week Mr. Tubie had told Darren, the other salesperson, that he could have the day off. But he forgot and got very angry with Darren when he didn't come to work. Darren told Julia that he does not like Mr. Tubie now. Mr. Tubie also forgot to reorder swimming goggles when the supply ran low.

Julia carefully closed the back door and entered the store to find Mr. Tubie to tell him. Mr. Tubie wasn't working that afternoon. Just Darren was there. She liked Darren OK, but he was weird to her. He acted unfriendly to her, and he was quick to blame her if something went wrong. She didn't know why he was weird. He said he didn't know anything about the back door.

That afternoon there were many customers. Julia and Darren could barely keep up with so many people in the store. Julia sold many things, including four pairs of "Air Jordan" basketball shoes because the basketball season was beginning.

Her neighbor Sam even shopped that afternoon. He needed new shoelaces for his old pair of basketball shoes. He laughed nervously about only being able to afford new laces and not new shoes. He had to hurry though to get to practice at the high school gym. She knew the boy's team practiced every day from 3:15 to 4:30 P.M.

Julia was unable to find the right size shoelaces for Sam, so she had to go back to the storage room to look for extra laces. Stacked on shelves were all the extra sporting goods. Near the basketballs, she found the right size laces, but the color was wrong.

As she hunted for the laces, her eyes noticed a broken window in the storage room. She wondered if Darren had seen it. She reminded herself to tell Mr. Tubie about it tomorrow.

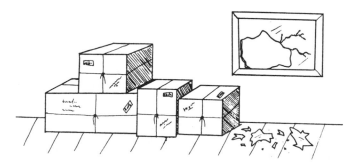

The next day at work Mr. Tubie was waiting for her. He was very upset. Someone stole three basketballs he told her. They were missing from yesterday. And he brought up the unlocked back door. "I don't know if you stole the basketballs," he said, "but you and Darren are responsible here. I'm calling the police."

That evening Julia and her parents called me at my office. They told me that they needed to hire a private detective because Julia was in trouble . . .

Use the **think sheet** on the following page to help you focus on giving *support* for your case.

Name_____

Think Sheet--Detective Report

1. What is your name as the detective? _____

_____

2. List all the possible suspects:_____

_____

_____

3. Whom do you think has the basketballs? _____

_____

4. What reasons do you have? Be specific. What hints are there?

_____

_____

_____

_____

5. Check which detective words you will use in your report to
   sound like a detective, or add your own.

   _____suspect   _____witness   _____testified

   _____stated   _____merchandise   _____stolen goods

   _____investigation   _____evidence   _____facts

6. What is a fragment?_____

STAGE TWO: WRITING THE FIRST DRAFT

Before you write your **first draft**, go back to page **52**, and read the **Police Report**. It will remind you of a detective's voice.

Copy this beginning of a detective report onto your own paper. Use your answer **#1** on the **think sheet** to fill in the blank name. Then use the rest of your **think sheet** answers as you write. Remember to skip lines as you carefully copy:

On Wednesday, December 5, at 8:33 P.M. I, Detective_____, received a telephone call from Julia X. and her parents stating their need to hire a private detective.

She told me that she was an employee of Tubie's Sporting Goods and that she was in trouble . . . .

Continue on and write a **sloppy copy** of the report. Use your answers **#s 2, 3,** and **4** from your **think sheet** in the report. **Expand** with anything you think is important to the case. Use detective words **(#5)** so that your readers will hear a detective's **voice**.

- Use a pencil.
- Skip every other line.
- Number each sentence after you finish.
- Write your ideas quickly.
- Don't stop for hard spellings. *Guess and Go.*
- Don't slow down now for perfect handwriting.
- Not every part of the report must be perfect.

STAGE THREE: REWRITING

Do you remember how to improve a draft by yourself? Read it to yourself listening and looking for ways you want to make your detective report better.

Another way to help your own draft get better is to answer this **checklist**. Then try to improve the points that you feel are weak. Number one (1) is best.

Self Checklist			
1. I like my name for the detective.	1	2	3
2. My report sounds like a detective is talking.	1	2	3
3. I have this many reasons for choosing my suspect.	1	2	3
4. I have combined this many sentences.			
. . . using compound subjects	1	2	3
. . . using glue words	1	2	3
. . . using colorful words in a series	1	2	3
5. I have found this many sentence fragments.	1	2	3
6. I found this many missing commas.	1	2	3

Home Checklist

Another way to improve your detective report is to read it to someone at home. Families usually like to hear what you've done at school, so take the rough draft home and read it to an adult. Remind your listener that it is a rough draft or sloppy copy, it's not perfect, and you want some advice on making it better.

After you read it to someone at home, ask these questions:

1. Does it sound like me or a detective wrote it?
2. Which words sound like a detective?
3. Do I have good reasons to believe my suspect is guilty?
4. Which reasons did I give?
5. Are all my sentences complete?
6. Does some spelling need to be changed?

If you need to change your detective report, add what you want, cross out what you don't want, or move parts around. Rewrite the report neatly on fresh paper.

Ask your listener at home to sign your report at the bottom. Don't forget to return it to school.

STAGE FOUR: PUBLISHING

Practice reading your report as if you were a detective reading it to the Chief of Police. When you are ready, read it to the class or have an adult read it.

Stay Tuned

You will learn how to make a strong argument to your parents. Coming up next . . . persuasive writing.

Persuading

Oral Language into Writing

ROLE-PLAYING AN ARGUMENT

Listen to this argument between Sam and Dave, two friends in elementary school. It's Saturday morning. Dave has slept over at Sam's house, and they're watching TV.

"Great! It's time for the *Danger Mouse* cartoon show."

"No, Dave, let's watch *Wonder Dog.* It's better than *Danger Mouse*."

"No, *Wonder Dog* is boring. I already have the *Danger Mouse* channel."

"Listen, Davey, it's my house, and I like *Wonder Dog* better."

"I've already seen all the silly Wonder *Dog* cartoons."

"Well, I haven't, and don't touch my TV set."

"It's not your TV; it's your parents', and I'll tell them you're being mean to me again."

"Davey, don't be a baby. If you don't want to watch *Wonder Dog* with me, go and play with Jesse downstairs."

"Jesse is five years old! I'm not playing with him!"

"Then quit crabbing and watch this cartoon. Last night you got to choose the ice cream we had for a snack."

"That's because your dad made you let me decide."

"Davey, I really need to watch *Wonder Dog*. I'm doing my animal report at school on dogs, and I need some information."

"From a cartoon? I'm telling your mom you're being mean again."

"Be quiet. They're still sleeping."

"Tough. I'm waking them up."

Oral Activity 1: Sam argued to watch *Wonder Dog*. He gave Dave seven reasons for his choice. Can you name them?

Oral Activity 2: As you can tell, not all of Sam's reasons for watching *Wonder Dog* are very good.

1. Which of the seven reasons is the worst?
2. Why is it a bad reason?
3. For the rest of his reasons, tell if they are good reasons or bad ones. Be ready to tell why. You must be a good thinker here.
4. Do you think his parents will agree with him or Dave?

Giving Good Reasons to Support Your Opinion

Probably you have been in an argument with someone over something you wanted or believed. You probably tried to convince the other person that your way was *best*. Just like Sam, you would give **reasons** to the other person for going along with what you wanted. But when Sam tried to convince Dave to watch his cartoon show, only some of his reasons were *good ones*.

Here is another pair of friends disagreeing. This time it's at school during recess. Val got a new bounce ball for a birthday present and brought it to school because there are never enough balls to play with on the playground. Val wants to play alone throwing and catching the ball. Bo wants to play with the ball, too, but doesn't really like Val very much. Bo asks Val to throw the ball, Val says no, so Bo jumps high and takes the ball. Bo tries to throw the ball back to Val to play catch, but Val starts screaming.

Here comes the recess duty teacher. What will Val and Bo say to him?

Oral Activity 3: Your teacher will put you in a group to think of reasons for either Val's or Bo's side. After your group has thought of some good reasons, your teacher will ask some of you to role play the youngsters' arguing in front of the duty teacher. Discuss which reasons are real.

Simple Sentence Combining

COMBINING WITH PREDICATES

So far you have practiced using your **writer's vocabulary** skill of **combining** to connect short sentences into longer, more interesting ones. Remember how to make a compound subject?

> The **light bulb** and **washing machine** are inventions
> that make life easier.

In this chapter you will learn how to make **compound predicates**. The predicate is the **does** of the sentence. Read these two sentences about Rindy:

Doer   **Does**

Rindy   **opened** a bottle of diet cola.
Rindy   **poured** it into the dog's bowl.

Since Rindy is the subject of both sentences, we can **combine** them like this so Rindy is **doing two things** in one sentence:

> Rindy **opened** a bottle of diet cola and **poured** it into
> the dog's bowl.

In your **writer's vocabulary**, this is known as **subtracting** because the writer **took away** at least one of the repeated words--*Rindy.*

66

Practice 1: On a piece of paper, write the two predicates from each sentence. (The two things the subject is doing.)

1. Aunt Edna became tired of her name and changed it to Na.
2. I will always take my dishes to the sink and rinse them off.
3. Food left between teeth feeds bacteria and causes tooth decay.
4. Don strums his guitar and plays his drums.

Practice 2: Take some words from each column to build three sentences with compound predicates. Use **and** between the two predicates.

Example: Denise Dew ate gophers and got sick.

COLUMN 1	COLUMN 2	COLUMN 3
Subject **doer**	**Predicate** **does**	**Predicate** **does**
Denise Dew	**ate** gophers	**painted** a fence
My friend Jerzy	**washed** a wall	**got** a backache
Two turtles	**lifted** a tank	**swallowed** the clock
Marcel	**carried** the box	**got** sick
Little old me	**woke up** in the middle of the night	**discovered** gold

Practice 3: Write three sentences about Super Turkey that have compound predicates. Here's an example:

Super Turkey **bought jogging shoes** and **ran in a road race**.

1. _____

2. _____

3. _____

An Easy Composing Rule

CORRECTING FRAGMENTS

You know that some sentences have compound predicates, such as:

> Jesse **made** toast and **put** ketchup on it.

The **doer** is busy and **does** two things.

Some sentences have **simple predicates** like this one:

Jesse **made** toast.

or   Jesse **walks** his hamster to school.

or   I always **forget** to water the plants.

The **doer** only **does one** thing.

Some *sentences* have **no predicates** like these:

     Ernie.

or   My little buddy.

or   Our first President George Washington.

They have a **doer**, but there is no **does**. These *sentences* are not sentences at all. They are lowly **FRAGments**.

Practice 4: Write **S** for a sentence (that has both a subject and predicate), or write **F** for a fragment (that is missing one part).

1. Julia played basketball and worked at Tubie's Sporting Goods.
2. Julia played basketball.
3. Our cute new pooch Rudy.
4. Sallie Spree broke her arm falling out of our apple tree.
5. The amazing Tina Turner.
6. Ginger built a new fort.
7. Thunder and lightning in the sky.
8. Cesar won the $1,000,000 lottery.
9. Was riding on a skateboard.
10. The new Barbie was too expensive.

Practice 5: Fix these fragments by **expanding** with a simple, compound predicate for them. Give them a **does**.

1. My darling wife Sophie. (FRAGment)
   a. My darling wife Sophie _____.
   b. My darling wife Sophie _____ and _____.

2. Mr. Dibbs. (FRAGment)
   a. Mr. Dibbs _____.
   b. Mr. Dibbs _____ and _____.

3. Fourteen octopuses. (FRAGment)
   a. Fourteen octopuses _____.
   b. Fourteen octopuses _____ and _____ .

Writing with Style

USING PERSONAL VOICE IN WRITING

Voice is the sound the reader hears when reading. It is the writer talking. **Good voice** is genuine to the writer. It sounds right. It sounds honest. It sounds real. That is, it sounds *right*, *honest*, and *real*.

In **Chapter 3** you wrote a **Police Report** pretending to be a detective. You used words a detective would use, so you sounded like a detective. In this chapter you will write with *your most honest, personal voice--your true voice.*

Practice 6: Read these passages and listen to the voice you hear. Vote for which paragraph (**1**, **2**, or **3**) has the best **voice**. Support your opinion.

1. His dad told him that he was going to get a new job in another city. He knew that meant they were going to have to move again, but it still shocked him.

2. His dad took him aside to get him alone. He had a weird feeling that something was wrong. Then his dad game him the bad news. They had to move again, and he would lose his friends.

3. A new job in another city, his dad told him. Even before the tears started to sting his eyes, he pictured his friends. What would he say to them? How could he say good-bye?

70

Listening for the Author's Voice

Your teacher will read this personal narrative written by a 9th grader, Eric McGhee. Listen to hear his **voice**. The voice is unusual. Then answer the questions from **Practice 7**.

It was five years ago that this humble piece of wood and glue hurdled into my life. It was the beginning of my fourth grade year as I ran upstairs to the bathroom door and pounded vigorously on it. My mother was taking a bath and had her ears submerged under the water. However, I managed to pound loud enough for her to hear, but not hard enough to knock the door down.

"Yes," she said. I could hear her lifting her head out of the water.

"I want to play a stringed instrument."

"Wonderful," she said. "Which one?"

"I was thinking of a lower one. Like cello or bass."

My mother was, and still is, an avid lover of classical music, so she immediately said, "Well, cello sounds nice."

"Naw, too many people play cello. I want to play bass."

This, in the beginning, was the true reason I began bass. In later years I began to like the deep, mellow sound, the ability to play just about every type of music there is, including classical, but I can never deny the fact that I liked it in the beginning, and still do now, because of its uniqueness. The fact that I'm pretty good at it is irrelevant.

Violins are a dime a dozen, but basses are one in a million. Me and my bass, we're going places.

Practice 7: Answer these questions about the bass story.

1. Does the writer seem to **care** about his instrument?
2. What **words** are especially strong?
3. Does the writer seem **honestly** trying to talk to you?
4. Are any parts **funny**?
5. What do you think about the **ending**?

Voice in Written Words

Of course, it's not always possible to read your writing aloud to someone. Usually your writing will be read by someone without you there. So your *voice* must come out of the *written words*.

Practice 8: To write with a strong voice, you must feel involved with the writing. You must care about what you are writing. Read this paragraph about the loss of a puppy.

I'll never forget our puppy Pebbles. She was a cocker spaniel puppy that my mom got at work. She was the cutest puppy ever. We only had her for a few weeks. When I came home from Jason's house, my mom told me she was gone. We couldn't find her. My dad thinks she was stolen.

1. How would you feel about losing a pet?
2. Does the writer make you feel sad about her loss? How?
3. Does the writer seem to care about the story? Support your opinion.

Practice 9: Now you write about the same loss but this time with feeling. Make the reader believe you are honestly upset.

Major Writing Assignment
PERSUASIVE LETTER--PET ARGUMENT

STAGE ONE: PREWRITING

Student Learning Objectives

In this paper you will:

1. write **two paragraphs** in a letter.

2. give at least **two good reasons** for keeping the pet.

3. use a true, strong, personal **voice**.

4. **combine** sentences with **compound predicates**.

5. have no **fragments**.

Writing Prompt

Most eight and nine-year-olds love animals. Most of you would like to have at least one pet to take care of. In this assignment you will write a letter to your parents arguing for a new pet of your own, a pet that you want desperately to have. Your job is to persuade your parents to let you keep the pet.

Helpful Drills

Before you begin brainstorming, let's pretend you want a mongoose very, very much. You read the story "Rikki Tikki Tavi" in Rudyard Kipling's *The Jungle Book* and fell in love with mongooses.

So you want to talk your mom or dad into letting you have a mongoose. What good reasons are there to argue?

GOOD REASONS FOR OWNING A MONGOOSE

1. very loyal to its owner
2. cheap to care for
3. keeps snakes out of the yard
4. small size--doesn't take up room

Will your mom or dad now say, "Sure, of course, you can have a pet mongoose. Let's go to the pet store right now!" Or will the answer be: "A mongoose? Are you kidding? What about the problems?"

THE REASONS AGAINST OWNING A MONGOOSE

1. very sharp teeth
2. born killer
3. needs warm climate
4. vet bills--shots and checkups

Parents can think of many reasons against getting a pet, even if the pet is not as unusual as a mongoose. So you must have good reasons and be ready to answer the arguments against your having an animal. Read this sample letter about keeping a pet crocodile.

November 24, 1995

Dear Mom and Dad,

1. The best thing happened to me at Martha's house. 2. The cutest crocodile was swimming in the trench behind their yard. 3. The crocodile loves me! 4. I think it would make a great pet because it would keep the cats out of our yard. 5. It would also teach me responsibility when I feed it food.

6. I know you will think it's dangerous. 7. I promise always to wear gloves and watch my step. 8. For its home we can dig a pond in the yard behind the garage. 9. Please, can I keep it?

Love,

Tex

Practice 10: Write three reasons for **keeping a turtle** you found beside a pond in the park. Write three reasons a parent would have **against a pet parakeet**.

Think Sheet--Pet Argument Letter

1. What animal do you want to have for your pet?_____

2. Where would you get it?

___a. from a pet store
___b. followed me home
___c. from a friend
___d. _____

3. What are three good reasons for you to have this animal?

a. _____

_____

b. _____

_____

c. _____

_____

4. What arguments might your mom or dad use against this pet?
Look at some of the ideas listed. **Expand** with your own.
Pick three of the best:

Acho-o

___ a. noisy

___ b. causes allergies

___ c. huge appetite

___ d. sharp claws (or antlers, or hooves)

___ e. _____

___ f. _____

___ g. _____

___ h. _____

___ i. _____

___ j. _____

___ k. _____

5. For the three reasons against your pet, think of how you can
make your parent not so worried about it. Write them down.

Example:

d. sharp claws -- I'll spend my birthday money to pay the
vet to clip the claws short.

1. _____

_____

2. _____

_____

3. _____

_____

STAGE TWO: WRITING THE FIRST DRAFT

Now you will write a letter to your mom or dad arguing for your new pet. In the first paragraph use your answers from questions **1**, **2**, and **3**. You may choose the two best reasons in **#3**, or you may use all three of your reasons. In the second paragraph use answers **4** and **5**.

Remember as you write your first draft (**the sloppy copy**) to:

- Write quickly.
- Use a pencil.
- Skip every other line.
- *Guess and Go* on spelling.
- Not worry about perfect ideas.
- Number your sentences after finishing the draft.

STAGE THREE: REWRITING

Since parents can be very firm about new pets, it is best to **read your letter to yourself** to hear how it sounds. Change any parts you think need improving to support your animal choice.

- Change a reason--be more specific.
- Change the order of your reasons.
- Change some words to improve your honest voice.
- Correct a circled spelling word.

Sentence Opening Sheet

Here is another way to improve your letter. It's the **Sentence Opening Sheet**. It helps you to:

- find capital letter errors

- **combine** two sentences that have the same subject (**Hint**: Look to see if you repeat the same sentence beginnings. Try to vary your openings by **combining**.)

- fix a fragment that has a missing **doer** or **does**

Go back to the letter about the crocodile on page 75 and see how a **Sentence Opening Sheet** works.

FIRST 3 WORDS	# of WORDS PER SENTENCE
1. The best thing	9
2. The cutest crocodile	11
3. The crocodile loves	4
4. I think it	18
5. It would also	11
6. I know you	7
7. I promise always	10
8. For its home	14
9. Please, can I	5

Sentence Opening Sheet

Name_____

First three words per sentence	Number of words per sentence

In order to make the very best argument for your new pet, get some advice from your classmates. Your teacher will put you in a "group of four." Tell your partners what your pet choice is, and they will write down answers to the questions **#s1, 2,** and **3** for you.

1. What animal does the writer want? _____

2. What two reasons would you give to keep it?

_____

_____

_____

_____

3. What two reasons do you think a parent would have against it?

_____

_____

_____

_____

Now trade letters and let your partners read it to answer questions **#s 4, 5,** and **6**.

4. I rate the voice as   1   2   3   4   5
                              not real   ok   true

5. Any spelling circles you can help with?

6. Any fragments you can help fix?

You now have three **checklists** from your partners.
Read them and decide if any of the reasons for or against are
good ones you want to use. Add them to your letter. You may
remove any you no longer feel support your opinion.

Also, the **Sentence Opening Sheet** will help you spot these
common student problems.

Your **writer's vocabulary** skill of **combining** with help you to
revise a sloppy copy. Here are some items to check for:

1. If too many of your sentences begin with the same
openings, try **combining**. You want variety.

2. If most of your sentences are short and choppy,
you need to vary your sentence lengths by **combining**.

STAGE FOUR: PUBLISHING

After you have decided on any
improvements to your letter, copy
it over on a clean sheet of paper.

Put it in an envelope and either
mail it or deliver it yourself to your
mom or dad. As they read it, listen
to what they say. Be ready to tell
your classmates and teacher their
answer to your arguments for a new pet.

Stay Tuned

Soon you will be writing a personal narrative. A what?
Chapter 5 will teach you how to write one.

Oral Language into Writing

BUILD A CHARACTER

All stories have characters in them. Characters are people in a story who do things and speak to others. At the beginning of **Chapter 4**, the story about the argument had two characters: Sam and Dave. In **Chapter 3**, there was a detective story. Do you remember the names of the characters in it?

Oral Activity 1: Read about this famous animal character from the comics. Can you tell who it is?

LOOKS	ACTIONS	PERSONALITIES
1. chubby	sleeps in a box with a blanket	bored
2. orange with black stripes	always eating	selfish
3. big grin	teases his owner	lazy

Oral Activity 2: One of the most famous animal characters is **Snoopy**, the cute dog in *Peanuts*. Be able to tell two **looks**, two **actions**, and two **personalities**.

LOOKS	ACTIONS	PERSONALITIES
1. long ears	sleeps on dog-house roof	wants to be a writer
2.		
3.		

Oral Activity 3: Describe a character who is a doctor. Use your imagination.

LOOKS	ACTIONS	PERSONALITIES
1.		
2.		
3.		
4.		
5.		

Oral Activity 4: This time describe a character who is Y-O-U.

LOOKS	ACTIONS	PERSONALITIES
1.		
2.		
3.		
4.		
5.		

Simple Sentence Combining

COMPOUND SENTENCES

As you have already practiced, **sentence combining** is used by writers who want to improve their writing. Instead of using short, choppy sentences, they **combine** them into longer, more interesting ones.

In **Chapter 3**, you learned about **compound subjects**, two **doers**:

Garfield and **Snoopy** must be millionaires by now.

In **Chapter 4**, you **combined** sentences using **compound predicates** which have two **does**:

Alcohol **drugs** people and **harms** their health.

In this unit you will write **compound sentences**, two sentences joined with: **and**, **but**, and **or**. These words are called **connectors**. They connect two or more sentences.

Examples: (1) Fifteen hamsters hot-rodded to town.
    (2) They forgot to fill the car's tank.

    (1) Fifteen hamsters hot-rodded to town,
        but (2) they forgot to fill the car's tank.

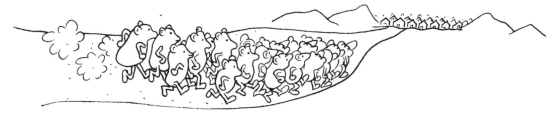

Notice: The period *after* town becomes a comma.
    The capital **T** in *they* becomes lower case.

Examples: Here are compound sentences joined with **and** and **or**.

(1) Jesse borrowed Sy's scooter, **and** (2) Sy didn't know it.

(1) The stars will shine tonight, **or** (2) the clouds will cover them.

Practice 1: What two sentences have been **combined**?

Example: Roger rode his exercise bike, and he listened to his Sony walkman.

    1. Roger rode his exercise bike.
    2. He listened to his Sony Walkman.

1. Pixie ate cheese, but Dixie wanted a salad.

2. My best friend Irma is moving to Ohio, and I'm lonesome already.

3. I'll write my story on the computer, or I'll use paper and pencil if all the computers are taken.

Punctuation Rule: A comma is placed **in front of** the connector word to **combine** two sentences into a compound sentence.

Practice 2: Match the short sentences in columns 1 and 2 to **combine** them using **and**, **but**, and **or**. Remember to place a comma in front of the connector words.

Column 1	Column 2
Deb eats all the fish.	It has been there a week.
My pet poodle better help me.	Kittie still hopes for some.
A strange car is parked nearby.	She gets no more soda pop.

Practice 3: Here are some short sentences that need to be **combined**. Expand with a sentence to go with them. **Make sure you add a sentence and not a lowly fragment**. Notice the comma in front of the connector words.

1. My dad has an electronic dictionary, **and**_____

   _____.

2. Spuds plays the drums, **but**_____.

3. I will go over there after school, **or**_____

   _____.

4. Jose scored the winning goal, **but**_____

   _____.

5. Little Billy raced home from school, **and**_____

   _____.

6. Rehana will work with her dad, **or**_____

   _____.

An Easy Composing Rule

USING QUOTATION MARKS

In many stories characters talk to each other. Authors put quotation marks ["] around the exact words the characters say. This is called **dialogue**.

"This birthday cake is ruined."

"Why are you dumping it into the greasy, gross garbage?"

"I used mayonnaise instead of frosting to ice the cake."

"Oh, no."

When the writer wants the reader to know which characters are talking, she will add words like:

she **said**   Little Lance **moaned**   **asked** his sister

Of course, no quotation marks go around these words because no character said them.

Whenever you switch to a new speaker, you begin a new paragraph.

A Short Story

Little Lance moaned, "This birthday cake is ruined."

"Why are you dumping it into the greasy, gross garbage?" asked his sister Jetta.

"I used mayonnaise instead of frosting to ice the cake."

Jetta slowly shook her head and said, "Oh, no."

QUOTATION MARKS

Practice 4: Here is a dialogue. Copy it onto your paper adding **quotation marks** where they belong.

The Drive

When Rico noticed that Leon was worried, he asked, What's with you?

Leon groaned, We'll never find a parking space.

Of course we will, Rico laughed.

How come you're so sure?

Smiling, Rico told him, It's 3:00 A.M.

Practice 5: In cartoons quotation marks are not used. Cartoonists use balloons instead. Read this cartoon:

Reprinted by permission of UFS, Inc.

Rewrite the cartoon using dialogue with quotation marks instead of balloons. Add words like *Jon said*. The first one is done for you.

"It says owners and their pets often look alike," Jon stated.

Writing with Style

USING ALLITERATION IN WRITING

Return to page **88** and reread **A Short Story** about the ruined birthday cake. Especially notice how Jetta described the garbage. In the beginning of this chapter, you wrote about Garfield. In the *Garfield* comic, the other pet that lives there is Odie, a **dopey, dull dog**.

In the *Peanuts* cartoon there is a little girl named Lucy who is **terribly talkative trouble traveling toward** Charlie Brown.

The words describing Odie all begin with a **d**, and
The words describing Lucy all begin with a **t**.

Such repeating of beginning consonant sounds is called **alliteration**. They sound good, and they're fun to write.

An 11-year-old named Kathy Redmond wrote a story about baking some *chocolaty, chocolate chip cookies*. Her classmate Nathan McKay described Ivan Drago, the Russian boxer, in the movie *Rocky IV* as a *humongous, massive mountain of muscle*.

Practice 6: Read these descriptions to find **alliteration**.

1. King Kong, an athletic able ape,
   climbed the building.

2. For lunch we had
   a powerful pigout
   on pepperoni pizza.

3. The moon was a silent sliver of satin hanging in the sky.

4. The dreamy, drifting draft of the air conditioner made me drop into a deep doze.

5. On Saturday I hated the hot, heavy, hilly hike.

Practice 7: Examples of **additional, all-star, awesome alliterations** follow. Match them to the three sentences below.

a. down in the dreary, dismal dumps

b. a huge hairy hassle

c. laughter turned into trickling tears.

1. Washing the dog turned into _____.

2. Wanda's bad mood put us_____.

3. Lynnie watched him until her_____.

Practice 8: Using the list of words below, write down as many **alliterations** as you can invent. You may change the endings of the words if you want or add more **gr**-words.

groan	grody	green	great	gritty
gross	groovy	groom	ground	grenade
grey	grieving	greedy	greasy	gravy
gravity	grapefruit	granola	grasshopper	grand

Major Writing Assignment

PERSONAL NARRATIVE: MY WORST ACCIDENT

STAGE ONE: PREWRITING

Student Learning Objectives

In this story you will:

1. tell the story about your worst **accident**.

2. use **quotation marks** for dialogue.

3. use other words for **said**.

4. **combine** 1 or 2 sentences into **compound sentences**.

5. avoid **FRAGments**.

6. write at least one **alliteration**.

7. use **colorful words**.

Writing Prompt

Have you ever had a *boo-boo* or an *owie* when you got hurt? Everyone has had an accident and has been injured. What does your family call injuries or accidents?

You are going to write a true story about an accident you had that caused an injury. Because the story really happened to you, it is called a **personal narrative**.

Practice 9: Before you begin to brainstorm your accident narrative, look at the picture. What might these characters say to each other?

How would you **feel** if you were in the picture, and you were the one who got hurt?

worried   scared   angry   nervous   embarrassed

Practice 10: With a partner tell your three strongest feelings if you had the accident in the picture.

Replacing *Said*

Whenever there is a conversation, words are *said*.

"Hi, Lupe," **said** Tobie.
"Hello, Tobie," **said** Lupe. "Where's your brother?"
"He's at the doctor's office," **said** Tobie.
"I need to give him his yo-yo," Lupe **said**.
"No problem. I'll give it to him," **said** Tobie.
"Ok, thanks," **said** Lupe. "I hope he's all right."

Gets a little boring, doesn't it? The word *said* is used too much.

Here are other words that can be used in place of *said*:

yelled	answered	responded	replied	asked
offered	whispered	inquired	exclaimed	declared
added	called	began	continued	

Practice 11: In the conversation between Lupe and Tobie, replace five of the six **saids** with words listed above. Of course, you may use your own word if you can think of one.

1.

2.

3.

4.

5.

Practice 12: Read this story about an accident. Notice that when the speaker changes, a new paragraph begins. How do you think it will end? Look out for editing errors.

Crash Landing

1. I always cut through Jamison Park to school. 2. It is a great shortcut because I save 2 minutes and 13 seconds, and I get to pass by Jolly Chand's house. 3. She has two dark, dangerous Doberman dogs in her fenced yard, and they go crazy whenever someone passes by.

4. Last Thursday the dogs surprised me. 5. they were very quiet when I walked by. 6. Too quiet. 7. Then I heard it: a very loud moan.

8. I peered over the fence to see one of the Dobermans lying on its side looking very sick.

9. I said, "hey, boy," to it. **10.** I noticed it didn't move. **11.** I yelled louder, "HEY, BOY!". **12.** I could tell it was in bad shape, so I ran to Jolly's front door to tell her that her dog was sick. **13.** On the second step to her porch, my foot landed on the edge, and I stumbled forward crashing onto the cement.

14. The cement porch hit my left knee, splitting it open in a second. **15.** Instantly, blood was everywhere, and I was screaming in pain and fear.

16. Jolly's dad opened the door, and screamed, "Oh, no, what is this?" He grabed me and draged me inside.

17. "Who are you?" I said as politely as possible with tears and blood dripping onto their carpet.

Short Writing Assignment

What do you think will happen? Make up the ending. Now write.

NAME ____

Think Sheet--Personal Narrative

1. Describe yourself. Use interesting **COLORFUL WORDS**.

LOOKS	ACTIONS	PERSONALITIES

2. Where were you when you had your accident? ____________

3. Who was with you? ____________________________________

____

4. What were you doing when the accident happened? _________

____

____

5. What is the first thing you said? _________________________

____

____

____

6. What other *said* words will you use?

_____

_____

_____

7. How did you feel? _____

_____

8. When you showed it to someone, how did he/she react to your

injury? _____

_____

_____

9. What were the worst and best things about your injury?

_____

_____

STAGE TWO: WRITING THE FIRST DRAFT

Following your completed **think sheet**, write a **first draft** of your personal narrative about your accident. If you remember something extra that happened to you while you're writing, use it even though it's not on the **think sheet**. You're **expanding**.

Remember: a first draft is only a first try, the **sloppy copy**.

- Write in pencil.
- Skip every other line.
- *Guess and Go* on hard spellings.
- Don't worry about perfect ideas.
- Write quickly.
- Don't worry about perfect neatness.

When you have finished your draft, **number each sentence**.

STAGE THREE: REWRITING

You have worked hard on your accident story, so it deserves to be polished up.

Rereading

With a pencil in your hand, **reread your story to yourself**. Read aloud softly marking any changes you want to make. For example:

- Check for any capital letter changes
- Replace some *saids*
- **Combine** some short sentences
- Vary sentence beginnings
- Put in quotation marks for conversation
- Make ending more surprising
- Improve your alliteration

98

Sentence Opening Sheet

This handy dandy chart was first used in **Chapter 4**. It helps writers find better ways to revise.

To review, go back to the story **Crash Landing** on page **94** to remember how to fill in the **SOS**. Can you see the sentences that need improvement?

Note: There is a new **SPECIAL** third column for *said* words.

FIRST THREE WORDS	# of words	SPECIAL
1. I always cut	8	
2. It is a	21	
3. She has two	19	
4. Last Thursday the	6	
5. they were very	8	
6. Too quiet	2	
7. Then I heard	8	
8. I peered over the	18	
9. I said, "hey, boy,"	6	said
10. It didn't move	3	
11. I yelled louder, "HEY	5	yelled
12. I could tell it	23	
13. On the second step	21	
14. The cement porch hit	13	
15. Instantly, blood was everywhere	12	
16. Jolly's dad opened the	19	screamed
17. "Who are you?" I	17	said

Your Turn with the Sentence Opening Sheet

Now it is your turn to use a **Sentence Opening Sheet** for your own accident story. Fill in the three columns for all your sentences. This will help you use your **writer's vocabulary**.

First Three Words	# of Words	Said Special

After you have reread your story and filled in the **SOS, read your story to your teacher** or **a classmate**. After listening carefully, your Editor will help you polish the story until it shines for publication.

Make any changes in your story that improve it, and then write your final copy. It should be your best possible work:

- better *said* words

- quotation marks

- at least one alliteration

- no FRAGments

- neat writing

- perfect spelling

STAGE FOUR: PUBLISHING

Make a second copy of your interesting, inviting injury story and give it to a partner. It is now a script for a play. Practice reading it until both of you are smooth and certain. Act it out for the class.

MINI-REVIEW TIME

- What are colorful words?

- What are similes? What does personification mean?

- Name your **writer's vocabulary** skills.

- If all your sentences are short and choppy, what **writer's vocabulary** skill should you use to make one sentence?

- What are glue words? Connectors?

- What is a fragment?

- What three words can you read before a *sentence* to see if it a fragment?

- In writing, what does *voice* mean?

- What type of *sheet* helps you gather your thoughts as you brainstorm?

- How does a **Sentence Opening Sheet** help you see problems on your sloppy copy?

- What different strategies can you try to revise a sloppy copy?

Stay Tuned

In the next chapter you will become your teacher's writing assistant. Here it comes . . .

Explaining

6

Oral Language into Writing

HOW-TO-DO-IT ORAL PRESENTATION

Have you ever explained to someone how to do something? Maybe you told a friend how to play a new game. Perhaps you showed somebody how to use your VCR or tape player. Did you ever help a classmate learn something new by telling him or her how to do it?

When you give directions, they need to be in a clear order, so that the listener can follow you easily.

Oral Activity 1: Explain to a partner how to make a peanut butter and jelly sandwich. Be sure to remember all the steps, including where to get the bread, peanut butter, and jelly, and what dishes and silverware you need. Try to explain the directions in the right order, so that you won't have to backtrack to tell a step you forgot.

Oral Activity 2: Now you will explain how to do something to the class in an oral presentation. You have a choice about what you will explain.

1. Explain to the class how **to do a chore**.

2. Explain to the class how **to organize something**.

Before you make your choice, take a few minutes to think of some possible chores. What chores have you done at home or school?

Now consider some possible things you know how to organize: your bedroom? your desk at school? a collection?

Make your choice, and prepare a short 1 or 2 minute talk or presentation to your classmates. Writing down a few notes on an index card is a good way to get ready.

What are some suggestions for speaking in front of the class? What do good speakers do?

Simple Sentence Combining

COMBINING WITH MORE GLUE WORDS

In **Chapter 2** you used your **writer's vocabulary** skill and **combined** sentences with **glue words**.

Do you remember how you used **before** to **combine** two sentences? **Combine** these two:

> You can make a peanut butter sandwich.
> You need to get the silverware.

You also learned how to use **after** to glue together sentences.

> I make my bed.
> I empty out the wastebasket.

Punctuation Rule

Hopefully, you remember that if the **glue word** is put at the beginning of the sentence, a comma separates the next part.

Here are two more **glue words** to use: **as**   **while**

They are used when two things **happen at the same time**.

> **While** Cesar cleaned the sink, Paul dusted the furniture.
> **As** I ate breakfast, Betty knocked over the prune juice.

Practice 1: Use **as** or **while** to **combine** these sentences.

1. You hold the pencil in the sharpener. You turn the handle.
   _____ you hold the pencil in the sharpener, you turn the handle.

2. I glue down the stamp. I hold the page firmly.

3. The garage door gets pushed open.
   The recycle box is carried to the street.

4. You write a first draft. You don't worry about perfect handwriting.

Practice 2: Use **as** or **while** to make up four sentences of your own. Remember commas if you need them.

1.

2.

3.

4.

Writing with Style

USING TRANSITION WORDS

Have you ever read directions? What do you think these directions are for?

First, stop working immediately. Stand up quickly and quietly. Next, walk to the classroom door. Then leave the classroom, walking in single file. Finally, get away from the building.

When writers want to be clear in writing directions, they need to use transition words. Re-read the directions above to find four transition words.

Here is a list of useful transition words:

• first	• second	• third	• fourth
• before	• as	• while	• after
• then	• next	• finally	• lastly

Can you think of any more transition words?

Transition words let the reader know the order of things. They are helpful in writing with style, but **not every sentence needs a transition word**.

Back in the fire drill directions, which sentence does not have a transition word?

Practice 3: Someone wrote this *how-to-do-it* paragraph on giving a dog a bath. Notice there are no transition words. In the blanks, fill in good transition words to make the directions easier to follow.

Washing the Dog

Washing a dog is a simple task if you follow these simple directions. _____, find a filthy dog. Coax it into the bathroom. _____ you fill the tub with warm water, talk gently to the pooch. _____ carefully lift it into the tub. _____wet down the dog before pouring a capful of the best shampoo into its fur. Using your fingertips, rub the shampoo deeply to get out all of the dirt. _____ rinse all the shampoo out of the fur. Find the softest, most expensive towel, and dry the fur completely. _____, give the dog a treat for being such a good sport. Oh, yes, you might want to clean up the bathroom a bit.

108

Practice 4: Sometimes a writer uses the same transition word over and over and over and over and over and over. Re-write this paragraph using some different transition words to replace too many *thens*.

Washing the Cat

First, find a pair of heavy, scratch-proof gloves, and put them on. Then get your bicycle helmet, and put it on, too. Then a pair of goggles should be worn. Then find Kitty. Promise that this won't take very long. Then fill the tub with warm water. Then very carefully put the cat into the water. Quickly rub a little shampoo into its fur, and quickly rinse it out. Then lift the cat out of the tub and dry its fur completely. Then let it go. Then put bandaids on any of your scratches.

Practice 5: Here are seven steps in the process of fixing a bowl of cereal for breakfast. First, write them in the correct order. Then add some transition words to make the directions clear. Use a colored pencil to write in the transition words.

Pour some milk over the cereal.
If you want it sweeter, sprinkle some sugar over it.
Go to the refrigerator.
Get a bowl and a spoon.
Put some cereal into the bowl.
Take the box of cereal you like out of the cupboard.
Take out the bottle of milk.

An Easy Composing Rule

USING COMMAS WITH TRANSITION WORDS

Usually transition words need a comma after them. Is that an easy composing rule or what?

Practice 6: Read these *how-to-do-it* directions, and tell where the commas should go.

Using the Card Catalog in a Library

First you must decide what information you need to find. Next notice where the card catalog drawers are located. If you know the author of a book, find the drawer that has the letter of the alphabet that begins the author's last name. Fourth look in that drawer until you find the card. You can also look for the title card if you know the book's title. Lastly you can look for a subject card.

COMMAS NOT NEEDED

The transition word **then** does not get a comma after it. Also, when the **glue words--after**, **before**, **as**, and **while**--begin a sentence, they do not get a comma behind them.

Practice 7: Make up three sentences starting with **first**, **next**, and **then**. Remember to use commas where they are needed.

1. First

2. Next

3. Then

Major Writing Assignment

EXPOSITORY WRITING: BEING A SUCCESSFUL WRITER

STAGE ONE: PREWRITING

Student Learning Objectives

In this paper you will:

1. write a memo to a student who will be in this class next year.

2. create a catchy opening to get the reader's attention.

3. explain the possible problems a writer might have and how to solve them.

4. use transition words.

5. punctuate sentences correctly.

Writing Prompt

You may not have thought about next year yet. However, your teacher probably has thought about how to teach next year's class to be better writers.

How about some help? Since you are now an expert at how to write in this class, you can share some advice to a student who will be in this class next year.

Write a memo to this future student explaining how to become a successful writer in this class. Your purpose is to help your teacher by explaining to this student some writing tips you've learned that will help her or him get off to a good start next year.

Helpful Drills

Practice 8: Look at this memo. Memo is short for *memorandum* which is a brief written statement that explains something. People in offices and schools send memos to each other when they need to explain something important quickly.

Read the following memo from an office worker to her co-worker. Be able to tell the steps she explained on how to use her computer.

Office Memo

Date: May 13, 1995
To: Phil
From: Mims

You are welcome to use my computer next week while I'm on vacation. It's quite simple to operate because it is very much like yours, but there are a few differences.

First, to start it up, reach behind the left side to find the switch. Be sure the plug is in the outlet! Second, you need to click on the program you want to use. After clicking there, go to the top of the screen and choose New. Next, you must set the page set-up.

Then you should be able to figure out the rest.

Good luck.

Practice 9:   To write a clear memo to someone, you first need to be clear in your mind on the steps to follow. For practice, list on your own paper the steps in how to use a pencil sharpener.

Short Writing Assignment

Write a memo to a friend asking for a favor. Your friend needs directions on how to get something important for you from your bedroom. Pick someone for this memo who has never been in your room.

Test your directions by sharing your memo with a partner to see that your instructions are clear. Check to see if your partner:

- understands the steps and
- can identify the transition words

Think Sheet

Now get ready to do your own **think sheet** in order to write the memo on being a successful writer.

Think Sheet--How to Become a Successful Writer

1. Describe some ways you learned to prewrite. Where do you get ideas?

   _____

   _____

2. What are some ways to organize your ideas to get ready to write a first draft?

   _____

   _____

3. What are some tips to follow when writing a first draft? What can a writer do to make the first draft easier to write?

   _____

   _____

4. Since good writers rewrite their first drafts to improve them, what advice can you give about rewriting? How can a writer fix a draft alone? With help?

   _____

   _____

5. What are some publishing ideas? What can a writer in this class do to share her or his polished final copy?

   _____

   _____

114

6. What are some problems a new kid might have with writing next year?

_____

_____

7. What advice do you have to solve these problems?

_____

_____

MEMO FORM

Date:

To:
From:

STAGE TWO: WRITING THE FIRST DRAFT

Following your completed **think sheet**, write a **first draft
(sloppy copy)** of your memo to next year's student.

Remember: a memo is longer than a note, but shorter than
a story or a report. Be brief, but be clear.

To help you pay attention to the important tips in your memo:

- *Guess and Go* on hard spellings.
- Write quickly.
- Don't worry about perfect neatness.

To help you rewrite your memo later:

- Write in pencil.
- Skip every other line.

STAGE THREE: REWRITING

Your advice memo is important to your teacher for next year,
so it should be as clear as possible. Now is the time to check it
over to improve any weak spots. You want it to be clear and
helpful to next year's student.

Rewriting Alone

Read your memo to yourself. On an index card, list what you told the student to do. Then as a little check-up list, use a different colored pencil to put a √ next to:

√ a tip for <u>prewriting</u>
√ a tip for <u>first drafting</u>
√ a tip for <u>rewriting</u>
√ a tip for <u>publishing</u>
√ any kind of <u>other tip</u>

Anything missing? If so, add the extra information your memo needs.

Sentence Opening Sheet

Now use the **SOS**. For this memo there are 3 columns to fill in.

First Three Words	# of Words Per Sentence	Transition Words

Column 3 is to check on transition words. Write down any transition word in each sentence. Did you use:

• first	• second	• third	• fourth
• before	• as	• while	• after
• then	• next	• finally	• lastly

If you did not use any transition words, can you go back to your first draft and add some to make your memo easier to follow?

Rewriting with Help

After you have re-read your memo and used the **SOS**, read it to a partner to find out if it:

- is clear
- makes sense and
- seems helpful.

Checklist Questions

After you read your draft memo to your partner, ask these checklist questions of him or her. Listen carefully to the answers. Make any changes that are necessary.

1. What did I just read to you?
2. Is there anything you do not understand?
3. What writing tips did you hear?
4. What one thing do you think you will remember?
5. Why do you think I read it to you?

STAGE FOUR: PUBLISHING

After listening to what this student tells you about your memo, make any changes in it to fix it up.   Write your final copy and give it to your teacher for next year's class. Thank you for your help!

Stay Tuned

In **Chapter 7** you will become a professional author. Find out how this amazing event will happen . . .

WHERE AUTHORS' IDEAS COME FROM

Many professional authors get ideas from real life -- things that happen to them, or to their children, or to other people they know or read about.

PRE-READING ACTIVITIES

Think--Pair--Share: Predicting

Your teacher will read you a story about a little boy who had many upsetting things happen to him on one day. Before listening to the story, take a moment to think what *might* have happened to him. Write your predictions on a piece of paper.

> Do you predict he will fall into a swimming pool?
> Will he get chased by a lion?
> Might he get stuck inside a box?

Next, pair up with a partner and tell your predictions. Be sure to listen to your partner's ideas, too.

Finally, your teacher will ask some of you to share your predictions with the whole class.

First Reading

As you listen to the story, write down on a listening sheet as many terrible, horrible, no good, very bad things that you hear in the story.

Choose your favorite event from the story, and draw an illustration for it. Why not share your reasons for selecting this event?

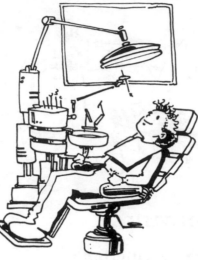

Re-Reading

Did you notice how the author, Judith Viorst, organized the story? Many upsetting things happened to Alexander in one day. Listen again to the story to hear what happened in the morning, during the day, and at night.

As you listen a second time, take your paper and mark your list in a time sequence:

- **M**   for events that happened in the morning

- **D**   for events that happened during the day (at school and after school)

- **N**   for events that happened at night at home

Major Writing Assignment

LITERATURE-BASED WRITING -- THE *NewTell*

STAGE ONE: PREWRITING

Student Learning Objectives

In this paper you will:

1. write a new version of *Alexander and the Terrible, Horrible, No Good, Very Bad Day*.
2. write in the first person (it is happening to you).
3. organize the day into three parts: in the morning, during the day, and at night.
4. use your sentence **combining** skills.
5. use synonyms for *bad*.
6. have no errors with paragraph indenting, FRAGments, and quotation marks.

Writing Prompt

Have you ever had a day when everything seemed to go wrong? Not serious problems like an illness or accident, but many little things that were annoying or upsetting?

Judith Viorst wrote a very successful children's book about Alexander and his upsetting day. You will take the author's idea and write your own version of a terrible, horrible, no good, very bad day. This is called a *NewTell* because you tell the story in a new way.

Remember that your story should be light and funny, not sad and serious. Everything in your story may not really have happened. As an author you can make up some parts of your story to make it more interesting to the readers.

Helpful Drill

Before you write your *NewTell*, you'll need many words that describe a bad day. Instead of using *bad* over and over, find some synonyms for *bad*. Judith Viorst gets you started:

- terrible   •   •   •

- horrible   •   •   •

-     •   •   •   •

Think Sheet

Use your **think sheet** to brainstorm ideas about your day.

Name_____

1. What does it mean to write a story *in the first person?*

   _____

2. When did your bad day occur? How old were you? Where did you live?

   _____

   _____

3. What went wrong in the morning? (List at least 3 things.)

   a.

   _____

   b.

   _____

   c.

   _____

4. How did you feel when these things happened? Use synonyms for *bad.*

   _____

5. What problems did you have during the day? (at least 3)

   a.

   _____

   b.

   _____

   c.

   _____

6. What were your feelings then?

_____

7. What bad things happened at night (at least 3)

    a.

_____

    b.

_____

    c.

_____

8. How did you feel about them?

_____

9. What were your thoughts at the end of this horrible day?

_____

_____

STAGE TWO: WRITING THE FIRST DRAFT

Use your **think sheet** to get some ideas flowing. Write your first draft without worrying about it being perfect. Plunge right into the action of your bad day just as Judith Viorst did.

Remember as you write your first draft (the **sloppy copy**) to:

- Write quickly.
- Use a pencil.
- Skip every other line.
- *Guess and Go* on spelling.
- Number your sentences after finishing the draft.

STAGE THREE: REWRITING

Professional authors try to read their first drafts just like someone who is reading the story for the first time. They try to hear how the story sounds to an audience.

EDITOR'S TABLE

One way to help a writer hear how her story sounds is to move to the **Editor's Table.** This is a place apart from where she wrote the story, so she can read it with *fresh eyes.*

Try moving to an **Editor's Table** away from where you wrote your first draft. Read the story softly to yourself listening to how it would sound to someone else reading it or hearing it. Mark any changes you think would make your story even better.

- think of another terrible, horrible thing that could have happened

- add more details--**expand**

- make sure you have events in the morning, during the day, and at night

- find a better word for *bad*

- **combine** some short sentences

- vary your sentence beginnings

Author's Writing Craft

Judith Viorst used a clever writing craft in her story *Alexander and the Terrible, Horrible, No Good, Very Bad Day.* She repeated the same line many times throughout the book.

What line did she repeat?

Why do you think she repeated that line so many times?

Re-read your story looking to see if you could use that same line in your story to improve how it sounds to a reader. Add that line wherever you think it would help make your reader be a part of the story.

STAGE FOUR: PUBLISHING

After you have made any changes to your first draft that will improve it, rewrite it into a final copy that:

- is neat
- is spelled correctly
- has no FRAGments
- has indents for new paragraphs
- uses quotation marks for dialogue

Maybe your class can arrange to visit a kindergarten, first grade, or second grade classroom in your school to read your stories to them. Be sure to rehearse reading your story before you visit. Practice reading with:

- **good expression**--make it sound interesting with your voice

- **eye contact**--look at your audience once in awhile and

- **proper speed**--don't be too pokey or read too fast.

Enjoy being a new author?

How about making a classroom library of your **NewTell** stories? Someone could be the librarian. Other students could volunteer to be assistants. Won't it be fun reading your classmates' stories?

Stay Tuned

The last chapter in **Check the Deck** turns you into an expert researcher. Onward . . .

Researching 8

Oral Language into Writing

BRAINSTORMING FACTS

In this last chapter of **Check the Deck**, you will be writing a research report about a subject you are interested in. Reports are often written in high school, middle school, or junior high. You've made progress this year in your writing, so let's learn how to write a research report.

We'll begin by brainstorming facts. This means to think of everything you know that is true about something. Brainstorming is letting your brain go free to think of ideas.

For example, here is a brainstormed list of facts about *cats*:

1. cats live about 10--20 years
2. babies are called kittens
3. some have long fur
4. some have short fur
5. like to sleep in the sun
6. famous mice catchers
7. have sharp claws
8. like to eat fish
9. climb trees to escape dogs
10. afraid of water

Of course, there are many more facts about cats. These facts were *brainstormed* (thought of) by some eight and nine-year-olds.

Oral Activity 1: With your class brainstorm facts that you know are true to add to this list about volcanoes.

1. Lava erupts from them.
2. Mt. St. Helens erupted in 1981.
3.
4.

Oral Activity 2: If volcanoes are not a familiar topic for you, how about one of these: dogs, horses, or fast food restaurants. Brainstorm facts about one of these topics.

Oral Activity 3: Brainstorm a list of facts with a partner about our planet Earth. Write down every fact you know about Earth.

After five minutes your teacher will ask one of you to read your list to the class.

Combining Facts into Sentences

SIMPLE SENTENCE

In a report, you must be able to **combine** the facts into interesting sentences. For example, let's look at these cat facts:

    3. some have long fur
    4. some have short fur

These two facts could be **combined** into one sentence in the report because they are **both about fur**:

Some cats have long fur, but some have short fur.

The connector word **but** is used to join them. This sounds better than:

Some cats have long fur. Some have short fur.

Two more facts could be **combined** in one sentence because they have **claws in common**:

    7. they have sharp claws
    9. climb trees to escape dogs

The **glue word because** can join them:

Because *they have sharp claws, they can climb trees to escape dogs.*

131

Practice 1: Use your **writer's vocabulary** skill and **combine** these facts about cats into one sentence. See if you can **combine** them in more than one way.

> **6.** famous mice catchers
>
> **8.** like to eat fish

Practice 2: **Combine** these facts about dinosaurs using the **boldfaced word**:

Use **but**:

> **1.** dinosaurs lived millions of years ago
>
> **2.** now they are extinct

Use **after**:

> **3.** dinosaurs laid eggs
>
> **4.** babies hatched like baby chicks

Use **adjectives in a series**:

> **5.** Tyrannosaurus was **tall**
>
> **6.** it was **fierce**
>
> **7.** always **hungry**

Practice 3: Here is a list of facts about planets. Decide which two facts belong together because they are both about the same thing or have something in common. Then **combine** them.

> **1.** astronomy is the study of planets
>
> **2.** planets circle the sun
>
> **3.** some planets are huge
>
> **4.** the path around the sun is called an orbit

An Easy Composing Rule

PARAGRAPH INDENTING

As you already know, paragraphs are groups of sentences about the same topic. Every time a writer begins to write about a new topic, he must begin a new paragraph.

Here is part of an article from the *Golden Book Encyclopedia*, 1960 edition, volume 12, p. 1108. It is about planets.

Some planets have moons. As the planets travel around the sun, their moons travel around them just as our moon travels around the earth.

Each planet has its own path around the sun. This path is called the planet's orbit.

Mercury travels faster than any of the other planets. It was named for the messenger of the gods. This planet is hard to see. It is so much closer than we are to the sun that it is usually lost in the sun's glare.

Practice 4: Answer these questions about the encyclopedia article.

1. What is the first paragraph about?
2. What is the second paragraph about?
3. What is the third paragraph about?
4. What do you notice about the first word in each sentence in all three paragraphs?

To help the reader follow his writing, the author of the article **indented** each new paragraph. That is, he moved the first word over from the margin. This alerts the reader that a new topic is being written.

Practice 5: Turn back to the story **The Ostrich in Love** in **Chapter 2,** pages **32-33**.

1. How many paragraphs are there in the story?
2. What is each one about?

Practice 6: Read this story about a cat. The writer forgot to **indent each new paragraph.** Where should he indent?

Meow Time

Dolores is a thirteen-year-old long-haired cat. She is calico, so her fur has three colors: black, brown, and specks of white on her neck and feet. Because she is a long-hair, her tail looks about ten times fatter than it really is. Dolores is lucky because she has her own door. In fact, she has two tiny doors. One was cut into the kitchen door that leads to the basement. The other door leads from the basement outside. She can come and go as she pleases.

Writing with Style

VOCABULARY BUILDING

A writer always has a choice of words to use. For example, here is a sentence about Dolores the cat:

Dolores has pretty fur.

To get a better picture, the writer chose a different word:

Dolores is a pretty **calico** cat.

The word **calico** describes her more fully than *pretty* because *calico* means **spotted colors**. The writer **expanded**.

Another writer wrote in a report:

The big dinosaur ate beside the water.

Here is another way to write about the same thing:

The big Tyrannosaurus ate beside the water.

The word **Tyrannosaurus** describes which kind of dinosaur, so the reader knows it's the terrible king of all the dinosaurs. What better word could you choose to replace these?

The **big** Tyrannosaurus **ate** beside the water.

These words are **synonyms**-- words that mean the same.

Practice 7: Replace the **boldfaced** words with better synonyms. Find synonyms for each word from sentences you have already read. Be sure not to change the meaning of the sentences.

1. Chi Chi **sits** on cooks.

2. The no-good band of rattlesnakes **went** over to the shopping mall.

3. Eric pounded **hard** on the bathroom door to tell his mom about playing the cello.

4. A **policeman** was hired to solve the case of Julia X.

5. I found the **people** of Borky Island to be **nice**.

6. On Monday the Ostrich **picked** violets for his beloved.

Practice 8: Write as many synonyms as you can for these tired-out words. Write them in a synonym wheel.

Example: small   Synonym Wheel

1. big

2. little

3. dumb

4. push

5. eat

6. good

7. run

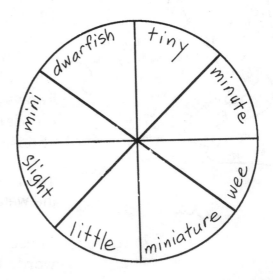

NEW AND INTERESTING WORDS

Another way to build vocabulary is to use new or interesting words you learn in your reading. For example, read this paragraph about dinosaurs (from the *Golden Book Encyclopedia*, Volume 5, 1960 edition, p. 421). Then go on to **Practice 9**.

Some of the plant-eating dinosaurs had armor
that helped to protect them from the flesh eaters.
Stegosaurus had a double row of plates down its
back and sharp spikes on its tail. Triceratops had
three horns and a frill of bone around its neck.

Practice 9: Write down at least three new or interesting words from the paragraph. Put a * next to your favorite word.

1.

2.

3.

Major Writing Assignment

RESEARCH WRITING--PLANETS or DINOSAURS

STAGE ONE: PREWRITING

Student Learning Objectives

In this report you will:

1. **combine** some facts into sentences.

2. write **two or three paragraphs** about a planet or dinosaur.

3. **indent** each paragraph.

4. use new **vocabulary** words.

5. avoid **FRAGments**.

Writing Prompt

Through class discussion and teacher directions, you have a choice of subjects for your research report: a **dinosaur** report or a **planet** report.

There are many **dinosaurs** to choose from:

stegosaurus	allosaurus	brontosaurus	triceratops
tyrannosaurus	trachodon	diplodocus	protoceratops
duckbill	styracosaurus	ankylosaurus	ornitholestes
thecodonts			

Here are the **planets** to choose from:

Mercury	Venus	Earth	Mars	Pluto
Jupiter	Saturn	Neptune	Uranus	

Practice 10: Brainstorm as many facts as you know to be true about your subject. Write them down in a list.

1. _____

2. _____

3. _____

4. _____

5. _____

Source

Now it is time to look for more facts about your subject. Where would you look to find more information?

Reading Your Sources

Once you locate a book or encyclopedia article about your subject, read it carefully to find interesting facts. Read this paragraph from *Dinosaur Story*, by Joanna Cole (William Morrow and Company, New York, 1974). Read carefully.

Brontosaurus dinosaurs may have stayed together in herds. When they ran, the smallest dinosaurs stayed in the middle of the herd. The biggest dinosaurs ran on the outside and protected the small ones from enemies.

What facts did you learn?

When you find an interesting fact, write it down, so you will remember it later. Instead of copying words exactly from the source, write the information using *your own words*. Write short phrases instead of copying long sentences.

For example, here are three facts written by a group of eight and nine-year-olds after carefully reading the paragraph on brontosaurus.

1. stayed in herds
2. babies running in middle
3. big ones outside for protection

Compare these notes to the paragraph. What differences do you find?

Practice 11: Take two notes from this paragraph on the planet Mars. Someone could volunteer to read this paragraph aloud.

The surface of Mars has nearly no water on it. There isn't even any ice. Its atmosphere, compared to earth, is airless. Instead of the combination of nitrogen, oxygen, argon, helium, neon, and carbon dioxide, Mars only has a thin atmosphere of carbon dioxide. The white clouds often surrounding Mars appear to be dust clouds.

Try to use your **own words** instead of copying exactly. Write in short phrases instead of sentences.

1. _____

2. _____

Practice 12: Here is another paragraph for more practice on note-taking. It is from the book *Wild and Wooly Mammoths* by Aliki (Thomas Y. Crowell Company, New York, 1977). Read it carefully to find two facts. Write them down using your own words instead of copying exactly.

> Imperial mammoths were not hairy. They didn't need to be. They lived in the warmest parts of the world. They lived in giant forests. Their teeth were flat, like those of the wooly mammoth--perfect to grind and crush leaves and twigs.

1. _____

2. _____

Think Sheet

Now read your source to find **ten facts** that interest you about your subject. Write them on a piece of paper in a list **using your own words** as much as you can. You do not have to write complete sentences for this brainstorming sheet.

Name_____

Think Sheet--Research Report

1. _____

2. _____

3. _____

4. _____

5. _____

6. _____

7. _____

8. _____

9. _____

10. _____

Here are some facts about the planet Saturn from *The World Book Encyclopedia of Science's* **The Heavens** (World Book, Inc., Chicago, 1987, pp. 114-116):

1. 6th furthest away from sun

2. takes 30 years to orbit sun

3. has rings

4. 885,200,000 miles away from sun

5. Galileo thought in 1610 that it had *ears*

6. Christian Hugyens in 1655 discovered rings

7. U.S. satellites discovered 4 more rings in 1979, 1980, 1981

These facts are about two different things: **distance from the sun** and **its rings**.

Practice 13: Let's put these notes into the two groups. The first four are grouped already. With your class, group the last three notes.

Distance from the sun	Its rings
1. 6th furthest away from the sun	**3.** has rings
2. takes 30 years to orbit sun	
4. 885,200,000 miles from the sun	

Practice 14: Here are some notes about the Tyrannosaurus dinosaur from the book *Dinosaurs and Their World*, by Laurence Pringle (Harcourt, Brace and World, Inc., New York, 1968, pp. 43-44). What are the notes about? Can you name the two groups? Sometimes *groups* are called *categories*.

GROUP A _____   **GROUP B** _____

biggest meat-eater ever   mouthful of sharp teeth
50 feet long   killed other dinosaurs for food
twenty feet tall   teeth 6 inches long
weighed over 8 tons   mainly ate duckbill dinosaurs

Practice 15: Read your notes about your subject. Ask yourself, *What are the notes about?* Think of two or three groups-- *categories*--they fit into.

Group   A   _____
Group   B   _____
Group   C   _____

STAGE TWO: WRITING THE FIRST DRAFT

In a research report the groups of notes are written into sentences that form paragraphs. For example, here is a paragraph that was written from the notes about **Saturn's rings**:

> Saturn is the planet with rings. In 1655
> Christian Hugyens discovered them, and in 1979,
> 1980, and 1981, U.S. space satellites found four
> more of them.

Look back to **Practice 13** on **page 109** to see if you can recognize which notes were used in writing this paragraph. Notice that two of the notes have been combined in the paragraph. What word **glues** them together?

144

Practice 16: As a warm-up, join a team of classmates to draft a paragraph about the Tyrannosaurus. Choose either Group A or Group B. Read the notes first, and then decide how to put them together into a paragraph. Select one student to write the team's paragraph. He or she should write in pencil and skip lines. **NOTE**: You may change the order of the notes.

Your Turn to Draft

Now it's your turn to write a first draft of your research report. Each group of notes will become a paragraph of facts about your subject. Remember:

- You may change the order of the notes.

- Try to **combine** some notes into sentences.

- Use new words and synonyms.

- Write in pencil.

- Skip every other line.

- *Guess and Go* on spelling.

STAGE THREE: REWRITING

Before you check your draft to make sure it is understandable to a reader, let's check a sample paragraph for practice.

Read this sample paragraph about a dinosaur and follow the five directions below:

The tyrannosaurus was a huge dinosaur.

It was the largest meat-eating animal that ever

lived. Tyrannosaurus stood over 20 feet tall and

was 50 feet in length. Eight tons was its weight!

PARAGRAPH RATING SCALE

PART I

1. Number each sentence.
2. Mark each note with a check.   (Look back to page **110**.)
3. Underline glue words and connectors.
4. Box new words and synonyms.   (Look back to pages **101-102**.)
5. Draw an arrow to the indent.

Here's what **Part I** should look like.

(1.)

→The tyrannosaurus was a huge dinosaur.

(2.) It was the largest meat-eating animal that ever

lived. (3.) Tyrannosaurus stood over 20 feet tall and

was 50 feet in length. (4.) Eight tons was its weight!

146

PART II

Number of sentences _____ x 5 pts.   = _____

Number of notes _____ x 3 pts.   = _____

Number of glue words _____ x 5 pts.   = _____

Number of new words from notes___ x10 pts.   = _____

Number of synonyms_____ x 10 pts.   = _____

Number of indents_____ x 8 pts.   = _____

                                   Total   _____

Your Turn

Read a paragraph from your first draft and mark it by following the five directions of the **paragraph rating scale**. Then add up the points. Did you beat the sample paragraph?

Now, mark and rate your other paragraph(s) the same way. Add up your score for all your paragraphs. If your score is too low, make changes to add points. Your teacher will score your report, too.

PARAGRAPH SELF-RATING SCALE

70-80 points	**WOW-WOW**
60-70 points	**GREATNESS**
50-60 points	**VERY GOOD**
40-50 points	**ADD a note, sentence, or a glue word**
30-40 points	**NEEDS IMPROVEMENT**

STAGE FOUR: PUBLISHING

After you have made any changes in your report to improve it, write a final copy. Remember:

- Your neatest handwriting

- Your best spelling

- Careful copying

This final copy should be your best work, so that you will be proud when someone reads it.

To make your report very appealing to the reader, you can also decorate it with a cover that has an illustration of your planet or dinosaur.

Ask your school's librarian or media specialist to display your report in the library for students to check out. You deserve to have your report shared with many students. You have worked hard this year on your writing. **Feel proud!**

Name_____

Beautiful   **Good**   **Needs Repair**

1. Uses **colorful words** to describe
    a neighborhood place.

2. Uses **similes** to describe
    something.

3. Uses **commas** correctly
    with **colorful words**
    in a series.

4. Makes me feel as though
    I am **vacationing** in your
    neighborhood place.

    Comment:

Solving a Problem Grading Sheet

Super Turkey   Keep it up!   Turkey weakling

1. The ideas follow a
    time order.

2. **Personification** included
    in the story.

3. Uses **glue word and colorful
    word** combinations.

4. Super Turkey **solves the
    problem** at the end
    of the story.

5. Makes me **interested** to learn
    more about Super Turkey.

    Comment:

Name_____

Detective Report Grading Sheet

Super Sleuth   Mm-EYE-ty good.   Asleep on the job

1. Names the thief and provides supporting **reasons** to convict him or her.

2. Sounds like a detective **voice** with the words.

3. Combines sentences with **compound subjects**.

4. Writes in complete sentences--**no fragments**.

5. Convinces me the next Sherlock Holmes has been found.

Comment:

151

Pet Argument Grading Sheet

You got it!   Getting better   Keep going

1. Writes at least **two good paragraphs** in the letter.

2. Gives **good, specific reasons** for keeping the pet.

3. Uses **true, personal voice** to persuade your parents.

4. Combines sentences with **compound predicates**.

5. Writes complete sentences-- **no fragments**.

6. Makes me agree to let him/her keep the pet.

Comment:

Name_____

<u>My Worst Accident Grading Sheet</u>

                                          Great   **Okay**   **Needs help**

1. Tells about your worst **accident**.

2. Organizes the ideas in
a time sequence.

3. Punctuates **quotation marks**
correctly.

4. Avoids *said* all the time.

5. Combines 1 or 2 sentences into
compound sentences.

6. Complete sentences--**no
fragments**.

7. **Alliteration** in the conversation.

8. Uses **colorful words**.

Comment:

Being a Successful Writer Grading Sheet

Terrific   Satisfactory   Rewrite

1.   Writes a **memo** to a student
who will be in this class next year.

2.   Creates a **catchy opening** to get
the reader's attention.

3.   Explains the possible **problems**
a writer might have and
provides **solutions** to solve them.

4.   Explains the **steps** that
a good writer follows.

5.   Uses **transition words**.

6.   **Punctuates** sentences correctly.

Comment:

Name_____

The *NewTell* Grading Sheet

Exciting **Interesting** **ReTell**

1. Writes a **new version** of *Alexander and the Terrible, Horrible, No Good, Very Bad Day.*

2. Writes in the **first person**.

3. Organizes the story in **three parts**: in the morning, during the day, and at night.

4. Uses **synonyms** for *bad.*

5. Uses your **sentence combining** skills.

6. **Have no errors** with FRAGments, quotation marks, or paragraph indenting.

Comments:

Name_____Date_____

SIX TRAITS OF WRITING	4 EX	3 VG	2 OK	1 NI
IDEAS: Clear and focused; holds reader's attention; specific amount of quality details; main ideas stand out; the reader gets a mental picture				
ORGANIZATION: Ideas and examples in an order *that is easy to follow*; logical; smooth transitions ; strong, inviting introduction; strong, satisfying conclusion				
SENTENCE FLUENCY: Sentences *glide* smoothly and naturally; variety of sentence beginnings, lengths, and structures				
WORD CHOICE: Words communicate message in an accurate and interesting way; varied and powerful verbs; imagery is strong; words are "just right"				
VOICE: appropriate voice for the topic; honest; written from the heart; words create a feeling or mood; writers "speaks to the audience"				
CONVENTIONS: Good grasp of standard writing conventions; correct punctuation, spelling, and capitalization; proper grammar and usage				

Overall Effect

Comment

_____Grade